Same Moon, Same Stars

The Life of Renate Macherauch Meiners

TOLD TO ELAINE THOMAS

Elaine Thomas

Same Moon, Same Stars
The Life of Renate Macherauch Meiners
Told to Elaine Thomas

Told to Elaine Thomas
La Grange, Texas
www.elainethomaswriter.com

Cover and interior design by Fred King, Houston, Texas
fking@2222dsgn.com

Printed and Bound in the United States
First Published in the United States 2014
ISBN 978-0-615-96743-1

Second Printing in the United States 2018
ISBN-13:
978-1986535809

ISBN-10:
1986535800

In memory of
my beloved
daughter, Evelyn

Preface

Hurricane Sandy's destructive path through the East Coast of the United States in October 2012, reminded me of conditions in Germany during 1944-1945. A hurricane's wrath is comparable to the aftermath of a war. Homes are demolished, voices cry out in pain and young mothers walk the streets, dazed, looking for their lost children.

But a war is manmade, not an act of nature. When I see war glorified, I grieve. If those who lived through a war had anything to say about it, there would be no more wars. My memories of World War II will never fade, but over time, I have tried to forget the bad and focus on the good that came out of that time for me and for my loved ones.

After a short article about my trip home to Germany in 1995 appeared in our local paper, The Fayette County Record, John Wied, who was district attorney of Fayette County, Texas, wrote me a note telling me I should write a book. At the time, I chuckled.

Only recently did I reconsider John's suggestion because those of us left who lived through World War II are old and frail. As a result, fewer first-person accounts are being written and those writing about the war now are using information they glean from various sources. I decided to provide a first-hand account of how the war affected an ordinary German girl growing up during Hitler's time. In years to come, perhaps my story will offer insight regarding that era.

Since the war, I have been asked, "Didn't you hate the Allies?"

My answer has always been, "No, they were people like us. It was wartime."

Had there been no World War II, I would not be in Fayette County today. I arrived in America as a war bride with my German-Texan husband, Harvey Meiners. Therefore, my life story also describes the tribulations that immigrants have faced for centuries. From confronting language barriers to dealing with homesickness and adjusting to a different way of life, it took time for me to adapt to American traditions and culture. Now I have deep roots here and do not wish to live anywhere else.

I spent many pleasant afternoons sitting at my kitchen table recounting my memories to Elaine Thomas. Retelling the early events of my life was not simple because I recall my youth in Germany in German.

I had to translate each anecdote and description into English for Elaine because she speaks no German. Sometimes finding the correct words or phrases was a challenge. After I came to America, I remember my past in the English language so those discussions were much easier for me.

Elaine is a good writer and I am grateful for her patience, skill and professionalism, as well as her friendship. When she read me the first pages of this book, I was moved to tears because Elaine had seen into my heart.

To the best of my ability at the age of 87, I have accurately and truthfully described the events of my life without the benefit of diaries or comprehensive notes to refer back to because none exist. If this book unwittingly contains errors, I apologize. I have done my best.

I could write another volume of fond stories about my daughter, Evelyn, who passed away from cancer on February 3, 2013. I loved her deeply and my life will never be the same without her. My beloved husband, Harvey, predeceased her in 2004.

As I look back over my lifetime, I give thanks to God. He has always helped me, especially during the most difficult days and He sustains me still. I am grateful for His grace.

Renate Meiners
Round Top, Texas
October 1, 2013

Table of Contents

German Words and Their Meanings

Bleyle – style of wool dress from a store by the same name

Christkind – Christ Child

Der – the

Frau – Mrs.

Fraeulein - Miss

Griesbrei – hot cereal

Herr – Mr.

Jungmaedel – Organization of Young German Girls

Kurrentschrift – Old form of German handwriting

Kristallnacht – "Night of the Broken Glass," the 9th and 10th of November 1938, when Jewish businesses were attacked in planned raids

Lebenslicht – candle representing the flame of life

Lieber Gott – Benevolent God

Onkel – uncle

Oma – grandmother

Postauto – mail carriers' vehicle

Sachs and Berlowitz – Jewish-owned clothing store in Weimar, Germany

Schwarzkopf – brand of shampoo

Sankt Nikolaus - a gray-haired figure with flowing beard dressed like a bishop who brought gifts to good children on the 6th of December

Strasse - street

Suetterlin - another name for old-fashioned handwriting

Tante - aunt

Urgrossmutter - Great-Grandmother

Urururururgrossmutter - Great-Great-Great-Great-Grandmother

Volga Germans – Germans from the Black Sea region of Russia

Wochenschau – recent news events

Zuendblaettchen – cap explosives for toy guns

Relevant World War II Events

1933: Hitler became Chancellor of Germany.

1935: Hitler violated the terms of the World War I Treaty of Versailles by building a massive military force.

1936: The Rhineland was remilitarized by the German Army.

1938: Hitler annexed Austria.

1938: Hitler's troops occupied the German border regions of the Sudetenland.

1939: Germany invaded Czechoslovakia.

1939: Italy joined Germany as an ally prior to the invasion of Poland.

1939: Britain and France declared war on Germany after Hitler ordered the invasion of Poland.

1939: Hitler ordered the extermination of Jews, gypsies, homosexuals, the disabled, etc.

1940: Germany crushed Denmark, Norway, the Netherlands, Belgium, Luxembourg and France.

1940: In the Battle of Britain, German bombers battered British cities in an attempt to obtain British surrender before the United States entered the war.

1940: Italy declared war on the United Kingdom and France.

1941: The United States enacted the Lend-Lease program to "lend" cash-strapped Britain military equipment to fight Germany.

1941: Hitler broke the non-aggression pact with Stalin and invaded the Soviet Union.

1941: Hitler declared war on the United States.

1943: Hitler's behavior and judgment became increasingly erratic.

1944: The Allies invaded German-held France on D-Day, June 6.

1945: The Russians took the German capitol of Berlin and Hitler committed suicide by shooting himself and biting into a cyanide capsule.

1945: After Germany unconditionally surrendered to Allied Forces on May 7, the country was split into four zones: American, British, French and Russian.

Sources: en.wikipedia.org/wiki/World_War_II; http://wiki.answers.com/Q/Why_did_Hitler_invade_ Italy; http://en.wikipedia.org/wiki/Timeline_of_World_War_II_(1945); wiki.answers.com › ... › War and Military History › World War 2

LITHUANIA

BALTIC SEA

SOVIET

Königsberg

EAST

PRUSSIA

POLISH

Danzig

Allenstein

Köslin

POMMERN

Stettin

WARSAW

ODENBURG

Warthe R.

NIEDERSCHLESIEN

POLAND

Liegnitz

SCHLESIEN

BRESLAU

Oder

OBERSCHLESIEN

Ratibor

PRAGUE

Elbe R.

CZECHOSLOVAKIA

TRIA

VIENNA

HUNGARY

LEGEND

1. Weimar
2. Bad Berka
3. Erfurt
4. Gera
5. Munich
6. Fuerstenfeldbruck
7. Nurnberg
8. Bremen
9. Eschwege

GERMANY
ZONES OF OCCUPATION
1946

—‧—‧—	INTERNATIONAL BOUNDARY
—‧‧—‧‧—	STATE BOUNDARY, 1937
—‧—‧—	PROVINCE BOUNDARY, 1937
———	ZONE BOUNDARY
	U.S. FORWARD POSITIONS, V-E DAY
	AREA COVERED BY CARPET PLAN

0   20   40   60   80 MILES

CHAPTER I

Reflections

"Good morning. This is Dan Mueller and you're listening to KVLG/KBUK in La Grange, Texas. It's time for the morning edition of the birthday and anniversary show brought to you by Adamcik's Appliance & TV Center in La Grange. Happy birthday this fine October morning to Renate Meiners who is 87 years young."

I'm startled to hear my name. Then I smile to myself, wondering which of my friends called the radio station. I sip my first cup of coffee and try to listen to the local news, but my mind wonders.

So I am 87 today? How could this be? Yes, really, I am an old woman. I can't get over this.

I remember so clearly those last weeks of World War II in Germany when my grandmother called herself an old woman. Oma, Selma Kuenzel Schmidt, was 63 then. I was 18 at the time and she did seem very old to me then, but not now.

Through word of mouth, we heard she was out in the meadow cutting grass for her rabbits with a little scythe while the Allied fighter planes roared right over her head on daylight raids. We were told she paid no attention to them even though they were so low she could see the shapes of the pilots' heads and shoulders in their clear cockpits.

We sent word back scolding her, telling her she was foolish. She ought to stay in the house when she heard air raid sirens.

After six long years of war, my mother and I, like most German civilians, hated that sound. Our hearts first missed a beat and then they pounded. What destruction would we witness next? Even though we lived outside the industrialized core, there was nowhere in Germany to hide from the war. We were physically and mentally exhausted, sick of it. Oma shared our feelings, but she dismissed our appeals.

Oma was quite a bit shorter than I, a petite lady. She always wore a long, dark, woolen dress with a dark grey apron and a dark knitted or crocheted woolen shawl or cape in the shape of a half circle. Even in warm weather, I never saw her in short sleeves. She always had on stockings and knitted socks that she made herself. Her black shoes had thick soles. When she went outside, she tied a dark scarf around her head, knotting it under her chin. She put up her dark hair, which had very little grey, in a bun. Her eyes were brown like mine and she wore a pair of wire-rimmed glasses with a single lens. The other had fallen out.

"Why would the Americans machinegun an old woman like me?" she would say.

Oma was right. They never harmed her. The pilots of those fighters wanted to destroy strategic targets - railroad stations, fuel reserves and factories - that were the backbone of Nazi Germany. A small, solitary figure in a long black dress carrying a basket on her back on a country hillside didn't pique their interest.

But then again, Oma proved to be right about many things.

She sensed that despite being a rebellious, headstrong little girl, I might grow up to be a credit to my parents someday.

She said Germany would pay dearly for the terrible things rumored to be going on behind the walls of Buchenwald prison on the hill above her village and what that madman Hitler was doing.

She felt that if I loved my American GI and he was good to me, I should go with Harvey to his home in Texas.

She expressed that our darling daughter, Evelyn, would always be a great blessing to us.

She insisted I must always trust in God because He would watch over me, as He had always watched over her.

I was born Renate Lieselotte Macherauch on the 1st of October 1926, at home in Bad Berka, a resort town with a population of about 6,000 located 12 kilometers from Weimar, Germany, a city famous for its cultural heritage. My mother, Anna Marie Schmidt, was 27 years younger than my father, Johann Ernst Macherauch, who was a widower when they met. I am their only child.

My father had a green thumb and was such a good businessman that he built up a successful nursery business and an experimental farm in Legefeld. He also owned a substantial three-story house constructed of native stone and half timbers there. He even produced a sales catalogue featuring his rootstock for pear and apple trees, strawberries - his favorite fruit, loganberries and many different varieties of gooseberries. They were exported to countries as far away as Canada. He shared his love of horticulture by teaching at the University of Erfurt.

My father's Bad Berka weekend house was a two-story home also built of native stone. He enjoyed his quiet retreat located in a valley at high elevation, although it was not in the mountains. Some years, Bad Berka had snow as early as October and when winter came it stayed, punctuated by blizzards and lots of ice. Christmas was always white and the winter air dry. Summers were very pleasant there.

My mother came from the small village of Troebsdorf, three kilometers from Weimar. At the age of 16, she began knitting scarfs and later socks for a wholesale store. This produced only a little income for her family. When she turned 18, Oma bought a treadle Singer sewing machine. Then my mother was able to bring work home from a garment factory. When she sewed precut sleeves and other pieces of clothing together, she was paid on the number of pieces she produced. But she still wasn't content.

Anxious to get out in the world, my mother applied to serve as a personal maid to 21-year-old Countess Alice von Medem, a German-speaking Russian, who lived in Weimar, Marienstrasse Number 11.

The Russian army had burned down 18 of the 19 buildings on the estate of Count von Medem in 1915 so the family had no home to return to in the Baltic country of Latvia. Nevertheless, huge gunnysacks of grain and potatoes and other food arrived regularly by train from their farmlands. That meant, unlike so many Germans, my mother never went hungry during the terrible recession following World War I.

After about a year in Weimar, my mother was asked to serve the widowed grandmother, Countess Julie von Medem, at Goethe Strasse in Dresden. She transferred from Weimar to the grand house along with a married couple, Herr and Frau Roesing.

Since a personal maid ranked higher in the household than a servant, my mother had a very good life in Dresden. At the time, Oma's cousin, Helene Jung, a famous soprano, performed with the opera in that city. Helene, who was two years older than my mother was, extended a standing invitation so my mother could attend Sunday morning rehearsals free. Afterward, my mother would rush back to cook dinner for the countess.

One Sunday when the potatoes weren't quite cooked, the elderly lady complained. My mother told her, "Those are new potatoes. That's why they are not soft." Such an original explanation kept my mother from getting into trouble.

While my mother worked in Dresden, her father, Eduard Louis

Schmidt, passed away on the 12th of October 1920. A draftsman by occupation, my grandfather designed modest homes and barns in the little village and the surrounding area. He had followed in the footsteps of his maternal grandfather, Julius Roeder; he had also collected taxes from the people for the ruler of the federal state of Thueringen, Count Carl August. My grandfather, who was 58 years of age when he died, was buried in Troebsdorf, the same village in which he had been born.

Like most of the people who lived in the country, my grandparents lived in the village and worked a small farm nearby that produced only enough feed for their animals. They also had a garden and sold what they didn't eat themselves once a week at the market in Weimar.

With no government assistance to help in those days, people had to make it on their own and family members were expected to help. My mother came home to help with the farm work on the 13th of June 1923 because my grandfather's death created a financial crisis for her family.

In the spring of 1925, my mother heard of an opening for a cook at the home of a retired gentleman in Bad Berka and applied. That's how she met my father. They soon fell in love. Around the time my parents were married, my father became ill with pleurisy. After my birth, he was diagnosed with tuberculosis. No cure existed.

I was baptized into the Evangelical Lutheran Church on the 4th of December 1926, by Pastor Schleifenheimer at the home of my parents. My sponsors were my mother's youngest brother, Onkel Max; my father's best friend, Wilfrid Dobers, M.D.; and Charlotte, my mother's friend from the House of Medem.

This is the only clear memory I have of my father. When I was a very small child, my mother must have been in the house while I played in our large backyard. We lived on a street corner. One street was very busy and the other, which faced the Ilm River, was quiet. Our yard had a wide strip of thick hazelnut bushes and lilacs so it was difficult for anyone to look in.

An old, bearded man dressed in a suit and hat sat on a wicker chair watching me. I mixed up some mud in my little pail and started painting the wheels of Mutti's little wagon. (Mutti was another name for "mom" in Germany.)

I must have gotten dirty because when my mother came outside, she called my name. That startled me so much that I ran into the open arms of the bearded man. I wanted to look at him closer, but he spun me around to face my mother. I recall feeling a little hesitant about that bearded man at first, but later I realized he was my father. Then I wasn't afraid of him. That is such a good memory to have.

Our yard was filled with more than 250 gooseberry bushes of five different varieties, although one was far tastier than the others were. We picked the gooseberries to eat, we picked them for jelly and we picked them to sell. For a while, my father operated a little business of making and selling preserves. This was a hobby for him. When he had retired earlier, he had given his oldest surviving son, Oswald, responsibility for the experimental farm and the nursery business.

I stayed apart from my father whose bedroom was downstairs. I slept in my mother's room upstairs in a single bed pushed against the slanted wall. Sometimes in the winter, my covers would be frozen to the wall because our house had no central heat, but that was not a hardship. I didn't know any better. We all lived that way.

Rosa Kahlo, whom I called Rosela, was a young unmarried woman in her 20s from Legefeld, who took care of me. My mother looked after my father. Another lady who lived nearby did the general housekeeping.

Not long after I turned three, my father died on the 24th of October 1929, at the age of 56. My mother locked the door to his bedroom and I was not allowed to enter it until many years later. That confused me because I didn't understand that my mother feared the room harbored tuberculosis germs that might make us sick. She never spoke of my father having suffered from tuberculosis. She only said he had been ill.

Every year after my father's death until I turned 16, my mother took me for x-rays at a sanatorium in Bad Berka to check for the development of tuberculosis. When the attendants turned out the lights to run the tests, my mother and a nurse would hold my arms down. I was very frightened because I was afraid of the dark. Fortunately, no one in our family other than my father developed tuberculosis.

Although my father may have thought he had made ample financial provision for my mother and me, the income was neither steady nor reliable after his death. That's why my mother rented out unused bedrooms in our house to earn extra money. We always had people living with us, whether they were vacationers during the summer or year-round boarders.

One day a knock sounded on the door. My mother took off her apron and answered it. A man was selling pencils door to door. He showed my mother and me his samples and they looked so pretty, but my mother didn't buy one.

r he left, I asked, "Mutti, why didn't you buy me a pencil?"

don't have any money," she told me.

Not understanding I asked, "Why don't you save money and then we'll always have some?"

What a thing for a child to say to a mother who was doing the best that she could.

Life in Bad Berka between World War I and World War II was comfortable. The church bells would ring at 6 o'clock each evening to remind us children of the curfew. Youngsters were not allowed to roam the streets, although they would have been safe doing so.

The stores were about a 20-minute walk from our home. When I went to the butcher shop with my mother, the butcher would cut off a slice of lunchmeat. He would then spear it with his big knife and reach over the counter to give it to me. At the shop where my mother bought her sugar and flour, I received a hard candy on each visit. It tasted so good.

Mutti did not allow me to have much candy and soda water because she said it wasn't good for my teeth. When I was given several pieces of candy, I had to give them to her. She would break off a piece each day for me until it was gone. My mother was right. My teeth are still good and I'm 87 years old.

As often as three times a week in the summer before I went to school, I would hear a bell and the sound of horses' hooves trotting down the road in front of our house. That was Herr Porter, a jolly Englishman passing by in his buggy. He operated the Wilhelmsburg Hotel, located not far from our house in the forest. He drove beautiful, beautiful horses. If he stopped and offered me a ride, I would run in and get Mutti's permission to accompany him as he did his shopping in town. When the war started, Herr Porter went back to England and I never knew what happened to him.

We used rainwater we caught off the roof in buckets to wash our woolens. We washed our hair in rainwater, too. There was no pollution to worry about. Laundry was not done as often as it is here – maybe once every three or four weeks. Underwear and other delicate clothing were washed out by hand on Mondays and dried outside on a clothesline. Solar power! During cold winters, wet clothes would freeze stiff as boards on the line. We would bring them back in the house and spread them out to thaw and dry on wooden rods on a rack that pulled out from above the kitchen stove. There were no paper goods such as towels, plates or napkins at that time. We each had a cloth handkerchief in our pockets and we each had our own washcloth, which were laundered weekly.

Friday was both fish day and cleaning day. There was always fresh fish to eat on Fridays even though we were Lutherans and had no dietary requirements. In the shop window was a fish tank. We chose the fish we wanted to buy. It would still be alive and the shopkeeper would kill and clean it before we took it home. Saturday was the day to clean house.

Mutti had a small oven in our kitchen stove, but she most often took her pound cake batter to the baker to bake. I recall carrying the cake tin with a clean dishcloth draped over it to town. I stuck my finger in and scooped out a taste. It was so good I didn't want to stop. When the cake was baked, it was much smaller than normal. I had eaten quite a lot of that wonderful, sweet batter!

While food was cooked in the kitchen, it was served in the living room. I recall that the kitchen was always warm. A huge avocado green colored tiled stove built into the wall of the living room heated three rooms. It burned wood and lignite, a soft dark brown coal.

When I was a child, I was well acquainted with all my Macherauch half-brothers and sisters except Hugo, who had died from pneumonia at the end of World War I, years before I was born. I was told he came back from the warfront with a horse and dog, both of whom were devoted to him. After his death, Hugo was buried in the Legefeld cemetery, not far from the family's home. His dog would not accept his master's death. Every time he got loose, he ran to the graveyard and began digging up Hugo's grave. The animal was inconsolable and had to be put down. Hugo must have been a man with high ideals. Before World War I, he helped German farmers gain more independence.

My eldest living half-brother, Oswald, who took over my father's business, did well for himself during World War II.

My half-sister, Helena, was good to me. Although she married, she never had children. But she would invite me to play at her house with her husband's nephew who was about the same age as me.

The baby of my father's first family was Wilhelm. He was about 13 years old when his mother died. His older brother sent him off to a boys' boarding school and Wilhelm always felt neglected. While still a boy, he immigrated to Canada in 1930. We became very close later in our lives.

Of all my half-brothers and sisters, Elisabeth, whom I nicknamed Peppi, was my favorite. I thought of her as "my Peppi" because she was so dear to me. I was 19 years younger than she.

When I was about four years old, she and her Austrian boyfriend, Erich Windbichler, would let me tag along on Sundays when they went swimming in Weimar. Peppi would take me by one hand, Erich would take me by the other, and we'd all swing our arms back and forth. When we got to the pool, I always had such a good time in the water. When I heard people say, "Don't let your child go unattended," I got a big kick out of shouting, "Hello, Mutti! Over here, Mutti!" My calling her mommy embarrassed her.

I was told that it was my father's wish that his daughters learn professions so we could support ourselves. Peppi, who was so easy-going and fun, had a mind of her own. She decided she wanted to marry Erich. My father must not have thought that being a sculptor and painter sounded like a promising career for a prospective son-in-law. Erich even dressed like an artist, a little different from men in business or professions. That is the one time I recall hearing that my father lost his temper. But in the end, Peppi followed her heart and my father forgave her before he died.

It seemed like everyone talked to me about my father when I was a child. It must have made a difference because when I visited his grave at Legefeld, often with Peppi, I would tell him what I had been doing. I felt that close to him.

Many years later, I came to understand that not everyone in the family was happy that my father had married my mother.

Mutti never spanked me when I misbehaved. Instead, she would cry and ask, "What would your father say if he knew what you've done?"

Rosela continued to help look after me for about four years after my father's death. One day, my mother had an appointment to get her hair cut before she went to the opera in Weimar with some other ladies. I decided to take care of my own hair with a pair of scissors. What a mess I made! Rosela had to take me to a real hairdresser for a real haircut to repair the damage as best she could. Little girls didn't wear short hair then except for Renate who cut hers off!

When I was five years old, my mother wanted me to give up sucking on a pacifier.

"They are for babies," she told me.

This wasn't a pacifier with a ring on it like those American babies use, but a pacifier on a bottle with a much smaller top. Mutti would stuff the top of it with a handkerchief and push in a cork so when I sucked, the bottle wouldn't collapse. I put a clean hanky on top of my pacifier in my apron pocket every day so I wouldn't lose it, but I often did.

I wouldn't leave Mutti alone. I demanded a new pacifier. Exasperated, she said I would have to go to the apothecary and buy it myself. She gave me the money and told me not to lose it. I put in my apron pocket and off I went.

The storekeeper asked me, "Whom do you buy the pacifier for?"

"I have a little brother," I lied.

"Oh," he replied, "I didn't know that."

When I came home, my mother asked me what Herr Geist had said.

"Nothing," I replied. Now I had lied twice and my lies were beginning to bother me. My mother had always taught me never to lie or steal. My family was God-fearing.

"If you tell a lie, der Liebe Gott will punish you," she said.

I didn't know how He would punish me, but I was afraid He might.

The next time I saw Oma alone, I asked, "How does God punish children who lie or steal?"

Unsmiling, she looked at me hard for several seconds before replying, "When they die, God makes one of their little hands grow out of the grave."

Oh, my, what a thing to tell a child! It finished me on sucking a pacifier. I gave it up for good. But the threat that I still would be punished stayed with me.

The next time Peppi and I went to visit my father's grave, I gazed all around the cemetery. I couldn't see a single hand sticking up.

Puzzled, I thought to myself, "Maybe they were all good children."

I felt comfortable in asking my Peppi anything so I inquired, "Does God punish children who lie or steal by making one of their hands grow out of the grave? Or does He forgive little children who are sorry?"

Peppi thought before answering. "Yes," she said. "God forgives those children who were truly sorry."

Then she told me to be more careful about what I said and did. What a relief that news was to me!

I was a child without brothers and sisters in the house, who always played more often with boys rather than girls. It wasn't my choice; it was because more boys were available as playmates. When I invited boys to come over to our yard, I would tell them to bring their own toys or a pet like a rabbit or a cat. I was bossy and they most often did what I said.

One time when a playmate's behavior didn't suit me, I refused to let him leave, locking the gate and throwing away the key. When the poor boy started crying, my mother came out to see what was wrong. My little playmate had diarrhea and needed to go to the bathroom, but I wouldn't let him. Back then, little boys wore short pants and it was obvious he had had an accident. Mutti had to clean him up before he could go home. Once again, my behavior made her cry.

Around that time, a worker was operating one of the first diesel-driven automatic tillers in our yard. It made so much noise that he attracted the attention of the neighborhood children. They stood at the fence watching the machine work. Excited at being the center of attention, I said a very bad thing and stuck out my tongue at them. Peppi gave me a swat and the other children laughed at me.

"You shouldn't do that!" she scolded.

I was embarrassed and felt awful because it was important to me what my Peppi thought.

An old man whose name was Herr Schiehl worked in our yard all summer. When he ate his lunch, he held a piece of sausage in one hand and a piece of bread in the other. First, he would take a bite of one and then a bite of the other. He would always ask me if I wanted something to eat. For kicks, I would tell him, "Yes," and he would cut off a little sausage and give me some of his bread. For my lunch, I, too, eat sausage out of one hand and bread from the other. It was so good!

Before the war, it was customary for a seamstress to come to our home to make my mother three new summer cotton dresses and sew nightgowns, aprons and dresses for me twice a year. I found it fascinating to watch the seamstress run a Singer treadle sewing machine. She warned me over and over not to put my fingers in the big wheel and get hurt.

When I was five years old, the seamstress finished my mother's dresses, but the sewing machine was still up because she planned to return the following day. Before Mutti left for town that afternoon, she told me not to touch it.

It so happened that the cat I'd brought home in my knapsack from Oma's house picked that time to have an accident. It stunk something terrible! I threw the cat out the window and cleaned up the mess on the living room floor the best I could with old newspapers from the wooden box next to the stove.

Then I'm not sure what possessed me. I marched upstairs and cut the back out of one of my mother's new dresses. I wanted the material to sew a pair of pants for my teddy bear. I didn't care about playing with dolls. I preferred my teddy bear. Of course, I didn't know what I was doing and the pants didn't turn out right. When my mother came home, I tried to distract her by telling her how I had cleaned up after the cat.

"What else have you been doing?" she inquired.

"My teddy bear needs clothes, too, so I wanted to make him a pair of pants."

"Where did you get the material?" Mutti said, looking worried.

"Well, it was here," I said, shrugging my shoulders and looking away.

She ran upstairs to check on her dresses and came back down holding the one I had cut up. I had made her cry again.

The following day when the seamstress came back, Mutti showed her what I had done. It cost my mother extra money to have a new piece of material sewed in the back of that dress.

Mutti never gave me a spanking, but perhaps she should have.

I learned my lesson. I wanted to learn to sew on the treadle machine so much, but Mutti wouldn't teach me. I never touched a sewing machine again until I was old enough to learn how to use it and had permission to do so.

I recall a visit to my Urgrossmutter (Great-Grandmother) Friedericke Kuenzel when I was about four years old. She lived in the village of Schoppendorf about three kilometers from Bad Berka with her youngest daughter, my Great-Tante Anna. To reach Schoppendorf, we had to cross the Hexenberg, which also was called Witch's Mountain. It was the highest point of the hills behind our town and legend had it that witches danced every night in a beautiful meadow at the peak, surrounded by many oak, birch and fir trees.

My mother would put me in a wagon and pull me along until we got to the foothills of the Hexenberg. From there, I had to walk because the pass was very narrow and very steep. Mutti was afraid that the wagon might over turn and I would get hurt. After crossing this pass, I would climb back in the little wagon again and Mutti would pull me through several more meadows before we came to my Urgrossmutter's little farm.

When we made this trip, Mutti would always tell me the story of Emilie, another legend handed down from generation to generation. Emilie was born in 1800 during the Napoleonic wars. Dressed in red uniforms and riding big horses, Napoleon's cavalry would plunder the little German villages in search of food. Each one, no matter how small, had a town crier, who watched and warned the villagers of impending danger. When a warning was sounded, they would hasten to gather up their chickens, goats, cats, dogs, swine and whatever food they on hand and load it on a wagon pulled by oxen. They would leave the village as fast as they could to hide in the Hexenberg meadow surrounded by the thick forest.

During one of these flights, 10-year-old Emilie performed a very brave deed. After the villagers had gone into hiding in the meadow, her mother realized she had left some food and animals behind. Thinking that Emilie was fleet of foot and small, her mother sent the little girl to fetch what had been forgotten. Emilie soon returned to announce that she had seen the last horses of Napoleon's army stampeding out of the village in a cloud of dust. It was safe for them to return to their homes. I loved to hear that story when we walked on Witch's Mountain. Emilie Heinel was my Urururgrossmutter (great-great-great-great-grandmother).

Urgrossmutter Kuenzel had white hair and wrinkled skin. She wore glasses, but still couldn't see well.

"Come closer," she would tell me. Then she would touch my hair and feel my hands to see if I was growing. She would ask my mother to thread needles for her and then push them into the arm of the chair so she could find them when she was ready to sew. I couldn't imagine how she could sew when she couldn't see.

Enthralled with the idea, I asked Mutti repeatedly, "Why don't you thread a needle for me?"

"I am afraid you will hurt yourself," she said. So that was that.

Great-Tante Anna would take me by the hand when she went outside to milk a goat so I could have fresh milk during our visit. I didn't like the way it tasted at all, but I never turned it down because I didn't want to hurt her feelings.

In the kitchen wall was a built-in chimney where they baked their bread. There was also a kitchen stove with a small oven that was used to dry out kindling. We were sitting in the living room one day when we began to smell something bad like burning hair. We rushed into the kitchen to find that two housecats had crawled into the open oven, curled up and gone to sleep. They were very comfortable, but the oven was still hot enough to scorch their fur!

There was quite a lot of forest left on the Hexenberg at that time. Each December, Onkel Max would go to the forester who worked for the government, to ask permission to cut down a Christmas tree. Although the land belonged to Oma, the forester had the responsibility of managing the number of trees that were harvested from the forest. Some years, he would allow trees to be cut and other years, he would not. There was nothing personal or political about his decision; the cutting down of trees had to be restricted because wood was still being used as a fuel for heating homes and cooking food.

In February following my eighth birthday, Urgrossmutter passed away at the age of 90. I was considered too young to go to the funeral. It was very cold outside and there had been so much snow that school had been cancelled. Since she had no babysitter for me, Mutti made an open-faced sandwich, cut it into little squares and poured me a glass of milk. She had made a nice fire in the stove so the kitchen was warm and comfortable. My mother warned me not to touch it while she was gone.

"Do you want me to tie the oven door shut?" Mutti asked me.

"Yes," I said. That way, I wouldn't be tempted.

I made myself comfortable in a big wicker chair in the kitchen in front of the window.

"Now you stay put," she told me as she went out the door.

I played with my toys and when I was hungry, I ate my snack. It may have taken Mutti an hour to walk to the funeral. The service may have been an hour or so long and then she would have had about an hour's trip back so I was alone for at least three hours. I behaved myself, though, and she was so happy.

I loved to visit Oma at Troebsdorf except I didn't like the outdoor toilet. It was nasty.

The original house, which had been built in the 1600s, was later turned into a barn. The rest of the house was built about 100 years later. Constructed of native rock, the walls were about 18 inches to two feet thick. Beautiful!

It fascinated me that the house and barn, which were built on a hill, were surrounded by a rock fence, too. Oma had her own water well. The pump was not very tall, but it had a long handle because the well was very deep. A bucket hooked to the pump caught the water.

A nice sized kitchen was inside the front door to the right. In the center of the kitchen wall, a two-foot square wooden door opened directly into the attached barn. The walls were so thick that there was room for a kerosene lamp to sit on the window ledge. If Oma heard a commotion in the barn at night, she would open that door in the kitchen and light the lamp to investigate the disturbance. Oma smoked her meats in a downstairs room. The bedrooms and the living room were upstairs. In the cellar, she stored potatoes and other root vegetables. She also made her own lye soap.

Each morning during the fair weather months, Oma would let her geese out of the wooden gate next to the barn. They would march one behind the other to the pond in the middle of the little village. There they would join other geese belonging to the 12 or 15 other houses that were close by. When I was five or six years old, I followed the geese to the pond because I wanted to know more about them. My mother let me go by myself, although she stood in the doorway watching me. How fascinating! I couldn't believe what I was seeing.

They swam around all day. Around feeding time in the late afternoon, the geese would swim to the edge of the pond, get out and form lines, marching one behind the other to their respective barns. At times, there would be three different rows of geese in the road. One row would turn off here, the other would turn off there, and one row would go straight ahead. I always liked to see that. I used to wonder how the geese knew which home they should return to in the evening. I still do.

Frau Henriette (Henni) Hieronemus, who lived on the corner in Oma's village, had snowy white hair and glasses. She would hang onto the burglar bars covering her low front window and call my name.

"Renatchen," she would shout. She was calling me Little Renate.

I didn't like that. In fact, I was a little afraid of Frau Hieronemus, although Oma often sent me to her house with a piece of cake she had baked. It took me a long time to realize that Frau Hieronemus was a good lady. Her husband was a quiet man whom I often saw working outside.

Oma would often prepare two big loaves of rye bread, about 13 inches in diameter. Her oven wasn't big enough to bake loaves that size so she put them in a basket and took them to the bakery. The baker knew whose bread was whose because each customer marked her bread with a different symbol. Oma's iron was an "S" for Schmidt in the middle of a horseshoe. The same brand, although larger, hung above the front door of the house. At the bakery, the bread would rise for a second time. Then the baker would take it out of the basket, load it onto a long shovel and put it in the oven. He would send it back to us in our own basket. Each family also had their initials on the outside of their basket. The baskets were washed and dried after each trip, ready for use again.

Every Friday and Saturday, the baker made big round cakes, about two feet in diameter, for his customers. Oma would bring a large round tray with a high lip to the bakery to pick up her cake and carry it home balanced on her head. The cake was stored on a rack between two bedrooms in the stairwell leading to the attic.

When I stayed with Oma, about 7 o'clock in the morning was cake eating time. We each got a pretty good-sized piece from the big round cake for our first breakfast. I always had milk to drink with it.

Our second breakfast at 9 o'clock was a little heavier. During the war, Oma gave me a slice of bread and a piece of homemade sausage, along with more milk to drink. In one hand, I held the bread and in the other, I held the sausage. I'd take a bite of one and then take a bite of the other, as I had seen the gardener do in our yard at Bad Berka.

Onkel Max had been married for a short time and then divorced. He had custody of his daughter, Inge, and they lived with Oma. Oma raised Inge. My uncle helped Oma with the animals and everything she needed to do because she was widowed.

I often talked Inge, who was six years younger than I was, into breaking off a little bite of cake at night. While the others slept, we ate more cake.

Oma made yeast cakes with sliced apples covered with raisins, sour cream, sugar and eggs. When prunes were plentiful, many of them ended up in cakes. Oma would start at the outside edge of the cake and put the prunes round and round in circles. It took forever for her to get to the center and finish decorating the cake. We would offer to help her, but we never did it right!

When no fruit was available, a specialty in our area was a cake that was made with locally grown onions. The yeast dough was covered in many layers of the thinly sliced onions smothered in real butter. Sour cream topped the cake. Even though it wasn't sweet, with so much butter, the cake was rich and tasty.

For afternoon coffee, Oma would break off more pieces of the big cake. She never sent us to get them. I wish she would have! She would ask another adult or go herself. The best pieces were those that were broken off right after the cake came from the bakery. Sometimes, the last pieces were a little dry, but we still had to eat them before they became moldy.

We ate off that cake all week long.

At my mother's home, the baker's delivery boy brought us fresh rolls each day except Sunday for our first breakfast. Mutti would hang a little sack on the outside door containing the correct change for the number of rolls she wanted to buy. Since he didn't come by on Sunday, she doubled up on her Saturday order. He arrived at about 7 o'clock, which was early for me to eat breakfast except when I went to school. Our second breakfast often consisted of butter and preserves spread on a good-sized slice of bread, which I enjoyed with milk. Every afternoon, we had cake or cookies. ☽

CHAPTER II

....

Treasured Childhood Tales

My mother enrolled me in kindergarten before I was six years old. I thought, "Now I will have other little girls to play with."

I was so excited, but I couldn't seem to behave. After lunch the first day, we were told to lie down on a cot and take a nap. We were told to be quiet, but I couldn't help myself. I bothered the little girl next to me and the teacher got upset. The second day, the teacher took my pillow, my cot and me out into the cloakroom. It was meant to be punishment, but I liked it in that room. I found it interesting. While I was supposed to be sleeping, I got up and switched all the coats around to different hangers. That caused a scene at the end of the afternoon when the children went to go home. On the third day, the teacher said she would have to speak to my mother.

She told my mother that the school had decided to dismiss me because I was such a difficult child. They didn't know what to do with me.

My mother cried again.

"You shouldn't do that," she told me through her tears.

It was too bad that I couldn't go to kindergarten any more, I suppose, but I didn't mind.

I was almost six and a half years old when I started school in 1933. There were three first grade classes with 25 to 28 children in each. On the second day of school, the teachers moved me from the first class into the second and on the third day; they moved me from the second into the third class of the same grade level because I was so disobedient.

My mother was horrified and cried when she heard what I had done.

"Why can't you behave?" she asked.

"I'm not going to do what the teacher tells me to do!" I told her.

I eventually did, although I wasn't always good.

School started after Easter and went year round until Maundy Thursday of the following year. We got six weeks off for summer vacation. Our school hours were from 8 o'clock to 1 o'clock except on Wednesday and Saturday afternoons, when we had classes from 3 to 5 o'clock. Saturday was devoted to playing games. We were taught reading, writing, arithmetic, drawing, history, geography and religion. Since I was brought up listening to classical music at home and always enjoyed it, I looked forward to Wednesday afternoons when we sang folk songs.

For the first three years, the teachers instructed us in learning a very old style of script handwriting called Kurrentschrift or Suetterlin. No one could help me and my mother told me repeatedly, "Try to do better." I always got a C grade because my handwriting tilted backwards. I was in too much of a hurry.

I have to admit it was so nice to go to school and play with girls. I didn't like one girl and she didn't like me either. One day when she got up to go to the blackboard, I stuck my foot out and tripped her. The teacher reprimanded me. When my mother heard about it she cried again, but I didn't feel very guilty.

Hans, the son of my mother's friend Tante Gretchen Sessinghaus from Weimar, taught me to crochet and then I got the measles. I would be upstairs in my room when my school friends would come to check on me. I'd open the window and talk to them while I crocheted a long chain. The girls would tell me, "A little bit longer, a little bit longer," and we'd all laugh. It took me two or three days before the chain was long enough for them to catch.

I made friends with a girl named Hannchen Sachse whose mother also ran a bed and breakfast a bit out of the way between our house and the school. She was my age or maybe a little older and fatherless like me. When her mother gave Hannchen permission to play with me, she would bring her dog. Before she crossed the street in front of our house, she would wrap him in a big blue tablecloth. I would march out into the street and stop the traffic on the main street - five cars perhaps. Then I would help Hannchen carry her dog across the street. When we opened the tablecloth on the ground, the dog would run out, ready to play. I lost track of my little friend when she moved away.

My family was staunch Lutheran, but that didn't keep me from taking a keen interest in the small Catholic Church in Bad Berka. I liked to go there with a friend, who was younger than I was, because I loved the smell of the incense and the quiet atmosphere. My regular presence was noted because when I was nine years old the priest came to my mother's house to tell her I was old enough to start confirmation classes. My mother was appalled. Needless to say, I didn't go to the Catholic Church any more.

After the third grade in 1935, I began to settle down. Until then my behavior was the lowest grade on the report card. By the time I was in the fifth grade, I was doing well in school.

A little boy in my class, who lived beyond our house near the forest, always looked dirty and didn't smell very good. No one in my class, including me, wanted to associate with him.

"When I see Rolf coming, I run so I don't have to walk beside him," I told my mother.

"You should not shun Rolf," she scolded.

"All the other kids do," I replied.

My mother explained to me that God protected Rolf the same way He protected me.

"Why would you want to do what the other children do? You should set a good example," she said.

From then on, I didn't run away from Rolf. I walked fast, though, when I saw him coming. Since I had long legs, sometimes he caught up with me, but most of the time he didn't. Rolf was drafted at age 16 and killed in the war.

During my school years, I read the book *Wiete erlebt Afrika* by Else Steub at least three times. This story of a girl's experiences in South-West Africa made me daydream. How it made me dream! I decided that when I grew up, I wanted to be a nurse on a luxury ocean liner that would take me to South-West Africa. If I found the country as interesting as Else described it, I would stay there. I hoped that Germany would reclaim South-West Africa as a colony so I could do that. By then, all books had to be approved by the government before they were purchased. I'm sure this title was approved because it reflected Hitler's plan to bring the colony back under German control.

We were taught in school that it wasn't fair for Germany to be stripped of its colonies like South-West Africa. It has been a colony of the German Empire from 1884 until 1915, before it was taken over by the Union of South Africa as part of the British Empire. South-West Africa was a huge territory, about one and a half times the size of the German Empire in Europe. Drawn by promising mining and farming opportunities, German people had settled there in large numbers.

I was confirmed on the 6th of April 1941, at the Marienkirche Church in Bad Berka by Pastor Heubel. Among the several dozen children in my class was a boy who had a very nice and very handsome older brother. I got in the habit of taking the long way home from the train station when I thought he might be on the same road. He would talk to me when others were not around, but he paid no attention to me when we were in a group. He was studying to be a teacher in the German colonies.

When I heard this, I told him, "I want to be a nurse or a teacher in the German colonies."

"You will need a very good education to do that and you must learn to play an instrument," he said.

My family welcomed my interest in playing an instrument so I got the cheapest instrument on the market – a guitar. I took two years of lessons from Fraeulein Schneider, who presented me with a Bible when I was confirmed.

"If I get a good education, I can do whatever I want," I thought to myself.

That's the way I felt. But I wasn't too preoccupied with political issues or the future. Like all children, I lived day-to-day.

The Sessinghaus family from Weimar visited us quite often. The father, Carl, who had been a friend of my father's, had a very good position with an optical company. From time to time, he would rent a room from my mother for a week to get away from the busy city. He was like a boarder, whose meals my mother prepared.

The family came to visit us in their car. That was big news for a child like me. I could sit in that vehicle parked in front of my mother's house. I don't think I ever rode in it, but they would let me sit in it. They had two sons. Heinz, the elder, was five years older than I was. The younger boy, Hans, was three years older than I was. He is the one who showed me how to crochet. Now and then, my mother would take me to Weimar and I would spend the night with the family.

Sometimes when I visited the Sessinghaus family, the boys and I bought little round caps of explosives called Zuendblaettchen that came in little triangle-shaped folded paper bags. The caps were very thin, even thinner than cardboard, and about half the size of an American dime. We'd put them on the streetcar track and run around the corner out of sight to watch for the streetcar. When it rolled over the caps, they would go, "Pop, pop, pop." We liked that sound.

Then the three of us would walk to the bakery and buy a big bag of cake crumbs before we went home. These were not my type of boys, though, because they wouldn't let me boss them around.

Tante Gretchen told my mother an unpleasant truth when I was about 12 years old. I overheard her say, "Renate will never amount to anything if she doesn't change her ways."

Those unkind words hurt my feelings, but deep down, I knew I was spoiled. I didn't know how to fix my own sandwich. I didn't know how to polish my own shoes. I didn't know how to make a fire. I couldn't do much for myself.

I give much credit to my Peppi for helping to straighten me out. I'm so grateful that she cared that much about me. I still could be difficult from time to time.

There was one more house behind ours and then there were wheat fields. I had to cross a wheat field to go to the Bad Berka pool where I learned to swim. I was allowed to go into the children's side where they always had lifeguards. Mutti didn't want me to take lessons because she feared I would drown, so when I was about 12 years old, I did so without her knowledge.

When I was 13 years old, I had to have one tooth on the left side of my mouth filled. During that era, the dentist would pump a pedal to run a big wheel to run the drill. He told me, "If I hurt you, raise your left arm."

I raised my left arm, but he wouldn't stop so I bit him. He was not happy. He stopped and then drilled a little more, packed the tooth and told me to come back the next day. That day, he drilled a little more, packed the tooth and sent me home again. The third day, after he filled the tooth, he got rid of me. Mutti wasn't proud of me once again.

I was 13 years old when my mother announced she planned to remarry. I resented this terribly. His full name was Hans Alfred Saenger, but to me he was Onkel Hans, the boarder who had roomed in our house since 1934. An accountant by trade, he came to Bad Berka to run a health spa for his father, a prominent businessman in Leipzig who had foreclosed on the business when the former owner wasn't able to repay a loan.

Those visiting the Bad Berka spa sought relief from rheumatism or digestive problems. The facility, which was supported by government health insurance, was comprised of three buildings. However, the mineral and mud baths and 12 guest rooms were the heart of the facility. Two masseurs and two masseuses lived in a little house on the grounds. Onkel Hans' sister, Elly, took care of the guests who were taking treatments. A commercial bottling facility on the premises produced two different flavors of mineral water.

Onkel Hans was a little shorter than my mother was and always wore a suit with a vest and a tie to work. In that era, the collars and cuffs on men's shirts were detachable. His shoes were always shined. He was a nice, mild mannered person, but he was to become my stepfather? What a shock!

On the morning of the wedding, Mutti instructed me to pick up my new dress from the seamstress. I could hear the church bells ringing when I left the house of the seamstress, but I had plenty of time to get to the church because she lived near it.

On the street, other children called to me, "Come Renate, let's go to the church."

A local custom called for newlyweds to throw pennies to the children when they came out of the church for good luck. My friends didn't want to miss that.

"I'm not interested," I said. I knew whose wedding it was and I didn't want to go. I took a long detour home and missed it. I got into trouble later, but it wasn't too bad. Mutti saw me crying.

After she remarried, I couldn't sleep in Mutti's room any longer. I didn't like that at all, but I had to accept it. My stepfather was still Onkel Hans to me until the day he died. He always was so good to me, though, and I came to love and respect him very much.

⋯⟡⋯⊚⋯⟡⋯

I have wonderful childhood memories of Christmas, Easter and Pentecost.

I looked forward to the Christmas season. Sankt Nikolaus often brought apples and nuts and checked to see if we had been good on the night of the 6th of December, Sankt Nikolaus Day. When I was 10 years old, my little friend, Siegfried, came to our house. Mutti told us to be very good and sit on the white bench against the wall in the kitchen. Under the wooden lid was a place for a washbasin, but that's where my mother stored her shoe polish. We kept our house shoes on a shelf on the bottom of the bench.

I thought Sankt Nikolaus must have started his visits to children in the village at our house because after dark, there was a very loud knock on the door. Siegfried crawled under the bench and huddled with the shoes, but I stayed seated looking very prim and proper. Then Siegfried began crying and my nose started bleeding with all the excitement.

Imagine our delight when my mother let in Sankt Nikolaus, whom we called "Der Nikolaus." He dressed like a bishop and carried a stick and a croaker sack - a big burlap bag filled with lots of apples. Then Der Nikolaus waved one of his sticks at us. We said a little prayer and told him we had been good children before he left. He had many more houses in Bad Berka to visit. How exciting!

Years later, I discovered Der Nikolaus was Siegfried's mother.

When I was about 12 years old, Siegfried's father told me, "I am your guardian."

I didn't know what to make of that statement. Did it have something to do with my father's will?

"When you are old enough, Renate, you will marry Siegfried," he told me.

I thought to myself, "Me marry that short little fellow who doesn't do what I tell him? No way."

I was positive that this marriage would not take place and it didn't. There were still a few arranged marriages at that time, but the custom was on its way out. I couldn't understand a mother telling her child, "You are going to marry this one or that one." Perhaps Siegfried's father said it for something to say. It was said with such assurance that I remember the conversation.

Mutti wanted me to go to Sunday school, especially after religion was taken out of our classes at school. Sunday school was okay, but if I met a school friend on the way doing something more interesting, I skipped it. Sometimes, I came home a little dirty and Mutti knew I hadn't been to Sunday school. When preparations for the Christmas pageant began in the late fall, my attendance record improved.

We presented our program at our church, which had very high ceilings, and was filled with people. In the building across the street, we took off our coats and changed into our white robes and halos. I liked being behind the altar before the program got underway. Some of the boys holding lighted candles got close to the girls with shoulder length hair and singed it. It would start to smell bad back there. It was customary for those of us who had longer hair to wear it in braids. My hair was thin and didn't grow fast. I made sure that my braids were in front so that wouldn't happen to me.

We gathered behind the altar where there was an open area and walked around to the front to face the congregation. The biggest angel carried an advent wreath with four candles on it. When I was 14 years old, I was appointed to lead the program and carry the wreath with the four candles. That was my dream, but when I came home from rehearsal, I had a high temperature. My mother sent for the doctor and I couldn't participate in the program. I had pneumonia. That was a dream I never realized.

Our program was always at night on the 24th of December. Then when we came home, the Christkind would have already brought us our gifts, which would be sitting under the tree, but not wrapped. It was not Sankt Nikolaus or Santa Claus who brought us these gifts; it was the Christkind.

Some years at Christmas, Mutti bought a tree. One year, she laid a little hatchet on the bottom of the wagon and covered it with burlap sacks. I wondered why she was pulling that heavy wagon when we were going to pick up cones in the deep forest not far from the Wilhelmsburg Hotel. Late in the afternoon, she went around some bushes and came back with a little tiny spruce that she put on the wagon and wrapped in the sacks. That was our Christmas tree that year.

Although I never saw it being done, our family's tree was decorated on the night of the 24th of December during the Christmas Eve church service. Some years, that was the job of Onkel Hans. Other years, my mother decorated the tree. That's why my mother came to the church service a little late. Our decorations, such as homemade butter cookies with a hole in the center, were very simple. There were also chocolate rings for ornaments, but no star on the top of the tree or garland on the branches. We had a few Christmas ornaments that we used each year. We later ate most of the decorations we made.

There were no presents for the adults. The thinking was that the adults could buy for themselves. Christmas gifts were only for children.

"Be good or the Christkind will not bring you anything," we were warned.

By the time I was 12 years old, I no longer believed in the Christkind, although I wasn't grown up yet. When I went to town, I always walked by the stationery store and looked in the window. I couldn't believe it when I saw a teddy bear on display. My old teddy bear experienced so many "surgeries" over the years he was worn out. When I went home, I talked about that blonde teddy bear and talked about that blonde teddy bear. I didn't want the Christkind to bring me anything but that teddy bear.

I kept mentioning it to Mutti, but her standard reply was, "Really?"

She didn't seem too interested. That didn't stop me from admiring the teddy bear every day. A week or 10 days before Christmas when I walked by, I noticed the teddy bear had disappeared.

I rushed home to tell Mutti the terrible news, "That teddy bear is gone!"

"Too bad," she said. "Maybe someday you'll have one like it,"

When I opened the door to the living room on Christmas Eve, there was my teddy bear. I was so happy!

That Christmas my mother must have had more money than usual because I also received a brand new pair of brown high top shoes with new ice skates. They were pointed rather than curled up in the front. I skated with my friends on the Ilm River near my mother's house.

We often had a goose for Christmas dinner that Onkel Max brought to us from Oma's house. I have a postcard Mutti wrote to Oma dated December 21st before she remarried. She asked if Oma could arrange to bring the goose to Bad Berka because Herr Saenger, (who later became my stepfather), was still living at her house and she needed to stay home and cook for him.

Also for Christmas dinner, we ate my mother's special potato dumplings, cooked cabbage and for dessert vanilla pudding with our own boysenberry syrup. In the afternoon, we enjoyed stollen bread, a yeast Christmas cake made with raisins, as well as some of the cookies from the Christmas tree.

Mutti soaked the stump of the Christmas tree in a bucket of water and often left it up until the 6th of January - Three Kings Day. On this date, we celebrated the Feast of the Epiphany when the three wise men visited Baby Jesus in the manger. Since the living room was closed off and not always heated, the tree stayed fresh a long time. Most of the heat in homes at the time came from the kitchen stoves. In the bedrooms, we had little heaters that burned lignite coal.

Easter was so nice, as well. Around the time I went to school, I recall using Easter grass - finely shredded green paper - to make a bird's nest. It was shaped almost flat to fit in my mother's wicker basket. When I went to put it out in our front yard, I looked for a rose bush that would cover and protect my nest in case it snowed that night. The next morning, I went out and looked in it. The Easter bunny had brought a papier-mâché egg filled with a little candy and hollow Easter bunnies. There was also a little apron in the basket and some boiled eggs! There were not too many colors; most were brown. Around the eggs little chick ornaments were nestled. My mother would go out and look at what the Easter bunny had brought some years. There were always eggs and once, I got a small wooden mechanical toy.

I didn't put my beautiful papier-mâché egg out again because it was so pretty and I didn't want it to get damp and spoiled. I have saved it all these years.

What we had as children is nothing compared to the way children celebrate Easter now, but I liked it. It had a lot of meaning for me.

We went to church on Easter Sunday and then we ate Easter dinner. Mutti prepared a leg of lamb from the butcher shop and, of course, her tasty potato dumplings. Easter was still cabbage time and so we ate cabbage. Although we had rutabagas, we didn't eat them at Easter. We had rutabaga soup instead. It was a nice family day.

Pentecost was a big celebration, too. Men and women did not celebrate together. From a small town like Bad Berka, the men would all go off together for a long walk, stop at a pub and eat their dinner. The pubs in those days in Germany were not like pubs here in the United States. They were more civilized. A few of the men played an instrument so they would play and have a good time. The women of Bad Berka would dress up and go to church with the children. Eating out wasn't common like it is now. In the afternoon, the ladies might go to a concert. ☽

CHAPTER III

In the Shadow of Nazi Germany

As Oma's cousin, Helene Jung, continued to build her reputation as an opera singer in the 1930s, she kept in touch with us. It impressed me that this diva entertained on a luxury ocean liner with her brother, Wilhelm, who played in the orchestra on the same ship. From 1931 to 1936, Helene performed at the Metropolitan Opera in New York. Whenever my mother received a postcard from Helene everyone would admire her, but to me, she always looked the same. It was her Pomeranian dog that became more beautiful each time I studied the cards.

As I grew up, I became more and more aware of the dictator Hitler and his Nazi Germany or Third Reich, as it was called. He came into power the year I started school. 1933 was also the year that the Nazis built Dachau prison.

The government issued my first identification card at the local police station in 1936 when I was 10 years old. Everyone was required to have an ID card and to show it when the authorities requested. The year before, Saarland, the sole part of Germany remaining under foreign occupation following World War I under the terms of the Treaty of Versailles, was returned.

After the third grade, Hitler saw to it that we received no more lessons in religion. Although I didn't realize it then, Hitler discouraged people from attending church by encouraging children to go to the movies on Sunday mornings. Of course, the movies were sponsored by the government so we didn't have to pay. I often took an extra roll with liver sausage in my lunchbox to eat there. That was my second breakfast.

Before the motion picture started each week, recent news happenings called Wochenschau were shown. Once a new film called *Olympia* by Leni Riefenstahl featured events from the 1936 Summer Olympics held in Berlin, including the 100-meter race. That was right down my alley. I loved to run so right then and there, I aspired to compete in the 1940 Olympics.

That must have been around the time I came home and announced to my mother that I didn't have to take a snack to school. Hitler had decided that schoolchildren should be served milk and rolls every morning. At a table set up on the lower floor of the school, ladies wearing white aprons served milk to every child who brought a metal cup from home. I wanted a metal cup to get some of that milk so much, but Mutti wouldn't hear of it. She didn't approve. She said we would buy our own milk and then put butter and jam on our rolls at home. My mother said Hitler was buying us; he wanted us to feel as if we were entitled to the food. That's how he gained the support of the German people, she said. I couldn't have cared less; I wanted to be like all the other children!

When I was almost 12 years old, I was standing at our garden gate with nothing to do, hoping that something good would come my way. A group of girls dressed in gym clothing, who were following their leader, marched past me singing. I recognized one of my school friends among the girls. They were on their way to a big sports field in Bad Berka. I wanted to go with them.

"They are members of the Jungmaedel, the Organization of German Girls," I told my mother. "I must join them!"

This Hitler youth program for girls from ages 10 to 14 looked like fun to me!

After joining the Jungmaedel, I was excused from Saturday afternoon classes. At school, we played handball and badminton, but I wasn't very good at either sport. In the Jungmaedel, I found I excelled at the 100-meter race. I always came in first in Bad Berka contests. I earned the opportunity to go to a county meet. I was told if I did well there, I would go on to the state competition. But I never achieved my dream of competing in the Olympics when I was 16 years old. In fact, I didn't even come close.

On the Saturday when I was to go to Weimar for the county meet, I asked Mutti to get me up very early so I could take the 6:30 train. She didn't and when I awoke at 6:30, the rain pelted down.

"Mutti, why didn't you wake me? Why, Mutti, why? I will be too late if I take the next train," I said.

"You see it raining hard don't you?" she said. "The competition will be canceled. There's no way it can be held outdoors on a day like this. I'm sure we'll hear when it's rescheduled."

I was very unhappy until I heard later in the day that the race was postponed for a whole year. A year later, it was cancelled for the duration of the war.

I still have the government requisition form for a new set of gym clothing stamped with the swastika, the symbol of the National Socialist (Workers) Party or Nazi party, as it was called. The shirt was supposed to have the Olympic logo on the pocket, but Onkel Hans said I didn't need it. He never signed that requisition. He wanted as little to do with the Nazi party as possible.

In the Jungmaedel, we sang German songs like the national anthem, *Deutschland Ueber Alles*. On cold or rainy days, we made small handcrafts. We stood out among the students in our class picture because we wore light brown uniforms with white shirts and ties. When we played sports, we wore matching short gym pants and short-sleeved jackets in the summer and long gym pants and long sleeved jackets in the winter. I was still a child and didn't connect all my fun with the Nazi party.

In 1938, when Mutti had two rooms to rent, she received a referral for a gentleman, Herr Luederitz and his daughter, Sigrid, who was my age. She was a beautiful playmate who filled the void that was left after my friend, Hannchen, moved away. Sigrid loved animals as much as I did and we spent many happy hours stroking her rabbit, which lived in a hutch in the backyard, and picking special grasses for it to eat. I enjoyed having cats for pets, but something always happened to them.

Also in 1938, Peppi's husband asked if I would like to pose for him. He wanted to sculpt a life-size male teacher with his arms around the shoulders of two students, a young boy holding schoolbooks and a girl with long braids holding a ball. I was that girl. I never met the teacher or the other child because Erich sculpted each of us individually. He worked with me off and on over a period of about six weeks. The swastika had to be part of the sculpture before it could be erected at a school in Eisenach.

All during this time, there were more and more references to the Fuehrer. The Fuehrer did this. The Fuehrer did that. The Fuehrer saw to it that we got a good breakfast. The Fuehrer wanted me to do this. The Fuehrer wanted you to do that. Everything nice the Fuehrer did for us. I would do anything that the Fuehrer wanted, but I wouldn't always do what my teacher told me. How did we know what the Fuehrer expected of us? Teachers and other authority figures informed us.

I told Oma what my teachers said.

"The Fuehrer gave me this and the Fuehrer gave me that."

She shook her head and said, "No, no."

Why was she being so difficult, I wondered? At home with my mother, there was no talk about the Fuehrer. She refused even to discuss him.

To me, the Fuehrer came right after God. That's how we children felt.

In the fifth grade, I had a teacher whom I admired so much that I told my mother, "He comes right after Adolph Hitler!"

They laughed hard when I said that. I will never forget that. I asked them much, much later why they laughed. They told me they were amazed at how Hitler had gotten the youth on his side and how much influence the Nazi party had on German children. I had no idea that I was buying into Hitler's propaganda. Mutti wasn't too concerned about it yet either.

While Adolph Hitler was like a god to me, God-Our-Father-in-Heaven came first. Oma made certain of that. She made sure we all understood that nobody was higher than God in Heaven was. She had some very strong beliefs. For example, when there was lightning, we had to sit with our hands folded in our laps so God would protect us. We couldn't eat food with our hands, nor pick up our tableware. Nothing.

In March 1938, Hitler annexed Austria. As a child, I welcomed this news because I had been told that Austria belonged with our German-speaking people.

In September 1938, Hitler turned his attention to the three million Germans living in the Sudetenland, an area in the northern Czech Republic along the Polish border.

Recognizing that Germany had become more and more aggressive, British Prime Minister Neville Chamberlain attempted to resolve the crisis by meeting with Hitler at his private mountain retreat in Berchtesgaden. That was followed by another meeting at Godesberg a week later and still another in Munich on the 29th of September.

At Munich, Chamberlain negotiated an international agreement under the terms of which Hitler could have the Sudetenland in exchange for making no further demands for more land in Europe.

Chamberlain called the settlement, "Peace in our time."

So on the 1st of October 1938, German troops occupied the Sudetenland. Hitler had gotten what he wanted without firing a shot. Hitler was right in doing that, we thought. That was my 12th birthday and we had an extra-large celebration because this meant there would be no war.

In honor of my birthday, my sponsors, Onkel Max, Dr. Dober's wife, Charlotte, and her daughter, Camilla, as well as other relatives, came for cake and stayed for supper. Mutti brought out the customary wooden birthday wreath. It was about two inches wide and painted white with different colored flowers depicting the different number of years. The center candle represented lebenslicht – the flame of life. I received wonderful gifts that year – toys, clothing and books. It was a birthday celebration I would never forget.

Many of us children hero-worshipped Hitler for a few more weeks, but then came Kristallnacht, the Night of the Broken Glass. The streets in Nazi Germany and part of Austria were covered in broken glass from the smashed windows of Jewish-owned stores, buildings and synagogues. These planned attacks took place on the 9th and 10th of November 1938. The German authorities did nothing about it. Most German civilians, including my parents, thought Kristallnacht was awful.

I could not believe it. I didn't know the difference between Jews and the rest of us. The word "Jew" had never come up before. I had no idea what Hitler meant when he talked about "the Jewish people."

I asked Mutti, "How can people do that to other people?"

"It is the Nazis who are doing it," she told me.

Nazis? Who are these Nazis? I had no idea what she meant by Nazis. I thought it was one individual. Then my stepfather came home from work one day very agitated.

"How is your teacher treating you?" he asked.

"He is treating me fine," I said. My stepfather looked relieved.

My seventh and eighth grade teacher, who was the leader of the Nazi party in Bad Berka, had threatened my stepfather. He told Onkel Hans that if he didn't join the Nazi party, they would take away his business. And they were capable of doing that.

Onkel Hans rarely raised his voice, but he was angry about the warning.

Mutti started shaking.

"Not so loud, not so loud," she cried, "Somebody might hear you."

She ran to the kitchen door and opened it wide, sticking her head out to check and see if someone was eavesdropping. She was afraid that she and my stepfather would be sent to prison for criticizing the government. My mother and stepfather made me promise that I would never repeat what I heard discussed about the Nazi party at home to anyone, especially strangers.

I listened. I was scared. I didn't want my parents to disappear.

When I was in seventh grade, Hitler said every German schoolchild should research and present her family history at school. We were to study our genealogy in order for the Nazis to know who among us had Jewish bloodlines. The Macherauch family history had been published in a book by Onkel Hermann Stoss, who lived in Berlin. I never saw the book, but Peppi got some pages copied for me. When we presented our reports at school, they were reviewed and certified acceptable with a swastika stamp. Then we were allowed to bring them home. My mother wouldn't help me at all. Although we had no Jewish blood that we knew of, she was too frightened.

Onkel Hermann and Tante Lee lost their lives in one of the terrible 1942 air raids over Berlin. Years later, when I went to redo our family history, a copy of that book was not to be found. To this day, I have never seen it. It must have perished along with Onkel Hermann and Tante Lee.

There were Jews living amongst us in Bad Berka. Herr Sandmann sold linen goods like tablecloths, dishtowels and bath towels door to door. He wore a long, dark coat and carried his goods in a case on rollers. He would spread his samples out on the living room table for my mother to see.

When he came to see my family, Herr Sandmann always knocked on the front door, but not one particular day. He came around to the back of the house where he couldn't be seen.

"You are still here," my mother said to him.

I didn't know what she meant. I could hear Herr Sandmann and my mother talking, but they were being very careful.

"Yes," he said. "I wanted to tell you that my children have been taken by the Red Cross. They are being sent to England and I hope that we can go there, too. We have permission. I came to say goodbye."

My mother smiled and nodded. Then she said, "I'm sure you are hungry."

He didn't disagree so she cut a generous slice off one of her big four-pound loaves of bread. She covered it with jam and served it to him on a little board. In the summertime, my mother always had all the windows open. I remember seeing him standing outside the kitchen window eating that bread and looking haggard. I felt so sorry. It dawned on me that something wasn't right.

After Herr Sandmann left, I asked my mother, "Why didn't Herr Sandmann come to the front door today?"

"Because he is Jewish," is all she would say.

"What did those people do wrong?" I asked her.

Why were the Jews being treated differently? They were no different from us, as far as I could tell. I couldn't understand. I still wonder.

But Herr Sandmann had to leave Germany because he was Jewish. I had played with his children. I have never heard another word about the Sandmann family.

Not all the Jews in Germany were rounded up by the government and interned. My widowed English teacher, Frau Biesi, lived in our house occupying the room my stepfather had before he married my mother. My little music teacher in Bad Berka, Ella Margarete Schneider, and Oma's neighbor, Frau Hieronemus, also remained free. We were grateful they were not persecuted because those people were our friends.

After Austria was annexed, the Third Reich invited Austrian parents to send their children to Germany on a holiday. A family in Bad Berka with a small baby took in an Austrian girl with whom I played. We took the baby out into the fresh air in a carriage for an hour or so on nice days. I felt good about pushing the child around the park in the fancy baby carriage with my little friend. When we would stop by the office where Onkel Hans worked, he would give us each a bottle of the special mineral water bottled there. I liked the apple better than the boysenberry. We could not drink out of the bottle. That was a no-no. There were pink glasses for girls and blue ones for boys. The bottle and the glasses were set in a big basket and we carried them home with us. We were not allowed to drink the mineral water there. That was a no-no as well.

On September 1, 1939, Hitler invaded Poland.

When I would try to talk to my mother about Hitler, she would put her lips together to indicate that she had zipped up her lips. She wouldn't talk. She was very, very afraid. ✍

CHAPTER IV

The War Years

World War II began when Britain and France declared war on Germany on the 3rd of September 1939.

Many Germans believed that the war really was lost when Hitler overran Poland. Had he stopped after invading the Sudetenland, everything would have been fine. In the aftermath of that military offensive, everything **was** fine. Everybody had work. Unemployment was low. Times were good in Germany.

"Hitler is a madman," the people of Germany whispered to each other behind closed doors. They were afraid to talk about the government because those that were overheard saying the wrong thing would be picked up and transported to places like Buchenwald prison, which Hitler had built in 1937. People sent there might or might not come back.

When war was declared, Mutti was in bed with tonsillitis. She started crying when we were informed that we should plan to pick up our ration cards the following Monday.

"Why are you so upset, Mutti?" I asked.

"I am out of soap powder to wash clothes. We have no coffee. We are out of about everything. I haven't been well enough to go to the stores for a whole week. Now we'll get only what's rationed," she said.

I was so happy that I could function by myself while she was sick. I straightened up the pantry putting big bottles in the back and little bottles in the front like rows of soldiers. We bought spices in little containers, but stored staples like flour and sugar, which came in 10-pound sacks, in big containers. When my mother came downstairs and realized what I had done, she almost had a nervous breakdown. She couldn't even take a quick inventory because I had reorganized the entire pantry.

On Monday, we showed our identification at the police station and picked up our ration cards. This setup was put into place almost overnight. The amount of the rations was adequate at first, but changed almost every week when we went to collect them on Friday night or Saturday morning. When we used the ration stamps, we still paid money. If a stamp was for one pair of shoes, we got one pair of shoes, but all the shoes were alike. At first, we got a new pair of shoes once a year, but later on in the war, there were no more new shoes. People stood in line waiting for the stores to open so they would have a chance to use their ration cards before everything was gone. Often, there wasn't enough food and goods to go around even with ration cards.

Early in the war after the farmers plowed up their potatoes and gathered them, Mutti and I picked up those that were left and she stored them in the basement. We would never have thought of pulling a potato plant out of the ground, though. That would have been irresponsible.

I was much older when I realized that my mother traded on the black market now and then. When she had something extra that's where she got it. Once she traded a little silver tea set for food. Out of necessity, many family heirlooms changed hands that way.

There were far worse things than having to deal with ration cards and trading on the black market.

Oma's neighbors, Frau Hieronemus and her husband, had two sons. At the beginning of the war, the younger one volunteered to serve in the army, but they wouldn't take him because he was Jewish. When he got home, he hung himself in the barn. The oldest boy, who was mentally retarded, died in a sanatorium. None of us believed it was from natural causes. This was a very sad situation because the couple had no other children. Herr Hieronemus died two years later.

Six or eight months after the war started, a bomb dropped near us. I was still in the seventh grade and a group of us went on a field trip to see the damage caused by the little English bomb. It damaged one side of a barn in a nearby village, but the cows in the other side of the barn weren't hurt; they were in shock. Everybody laughed about it, but it soon wasn't funny.

My mother's brother, Onkel Rudi, was drafted in 1942 and his oldest son, Fritz, followed the next year. It was a shock to our family when both were killed in action on the Eastern Front. Onkel Arno, my mother's oldest brother, was not drafted. He had responsibility for the motor pool in Leuna, near Leipzig, the location of Nazi Germany's largest oil refinery. Despite heavy bombing of the facility, he survived the war. Onkel Max, who had very bad eyesight, was put to work in a parachute factory about 100 kilometers from home in 1943. He never wore a German army uniform, yet the authorities did not allow him to come home.

There was no old age pension in those days. Oma's income came mostly from selling rabbits or hawks and milking two cows. She found it hard to manage with Onkel Max gone because she couldn't do all that work by herself. My cousin, Inge, was still a small child. This caused my poor grandmother to suffer a nervous breakdown.

Mutti brought Oma and Inge to our house in Bad Berka and made a bed for the old lady in the living room. After the doctor examined Oma, he told my mother she might not live more than a day. Overhearing that frightened me. I loved Oma so much; I didn't want her to die. We prayed and prayed.

Little by little, Oma recovered until she had the strength to go back to her home. Her best friend and Jewish neighbor, Frau Hieronemus, the same lady who had once frightened me, helped her to carry on.

Oma often heard the sound of gunshots at night from Buchenwald prison. When I visited, I would often find her sitting on a little stool in front of her big wood burning tile stove with a book in her lap. In the wintertime, the stove's door would be wide open for heat.

"Hello, I am here," I would say and then she would tell me, "Something is happening. There is so much shooting going on at the prison. Whatever is going on up there isn't right and the German people will have to pay for it one day. God will punish us. It is wrong what they are doing."

When I went home, I told Mutti what Oma had said.

"Oh," my mother said, "I hope nothing happens to her."

Mutti was afraid that she would be turned in for criticizing the government.

When I went back to visit Oma again, I relayed my mother's fears. She said, "They're not going to do anything to me. What do they want with an old lady?"

Oma told me about an old couple from Weimar who went up the hill to Buchenwald prison and approached the guardhouse.

The gentleman told the guard, "We want to see what is going on here. We have heard rumors."

"Would you like to come in?" the guard asked.

The man said he would.

The guard went away to make arrangements. When he returned, he said, "You can come in, but not your wife. She must stay outside."

So the gentleman went into Buchenwald prison while his wife sat on the bench outside the guardhouse and waited. The afternoon went by and when it started to get dark, the wife took the last bus back home to Weimar.

What happened to her husband? No one knew. He was never seen or heard from again.

Herr Geist, who owned the stationary store in Bad Berka, must have said something wrong because he was taken to Buchenwald prison. He came back after about six weeks. People asked him in a roundabout way, "How was it?"

"Like any other jail," he replied. That's all he would say.

People were shocked when our church pastor was jailed for six weeks because he didn't mention the Fuehrer in his prayers at Sunday morning services. That was going a little bit too far. I never heard where the Nazis took him, but perhaps it was to Buchenwald prison, as well. He came back and after that, he always included the Fuehrer in his prayers.

Yes, there was something wrong with Hitler and his Nazis.

The business that Onkel Hans operated at the spa closed in 1939. His delivery driver was drafted and the truck he drove, a little Opel, was confiscated. Starting in 1941, the buildings were used by the Red Cross as a recuperating hospital for wounded German soldiers. Although Onkel Hans was drafted to work at a military office in Weimar, he came home every night on the train.

In spite of the war, life went on for young women like me.

Frau Biesi, one of the three teachers who lived in our house, wanted something to do so she offered to teach me English in secret. My stepfather was all for that. She furnished me with a book she had used during her teaching career that hadn't been destroyed by the Nazis. For two years, I took very private lessons from her and learned to read and speak the language a little bit, although she spoke with a little bit of an English accent and I picked it up, too.

I finished the eighth grade in 1941. Now what? All private schools had been closed until they had successfully converted over to the government's curriculum. There was a girls' school in Weimar I could attend, but first Hitler announced every young girl who grew up in the city should volunteer to experience farm life and every girl who grew up in the country should experience city life for one year.

Oh, yes, I was for that! I was very determined to get away from home.

My mother said, "No, no, no."

Perhaps one of the reasons that she decided to let me go because I was spoiled and we both knew it. I never polished a shoe. My mother did that. If we had a sandwich at night, my mother would cut the bread, put on the filling and serve it to me on a little board. My mother did everything for me.

My school friend, Ursel, and I were placed on good-sized farms near Merkendorf in Vogtland, two hours southeast of Bad Berka on a slow train. There, I was surprised to find a different kind of farm from Oma's few acres and small number of poultry and cows.

Working with a French prisoner on one side of me and a Russian prisoner on the other, I gathered potatoes from the big fields. Both men helped me, although it was not easy for us to communicate. The French prisoner felt sorry for me because he had a daughter at home who also was 15 years old. Part of my responsibility was cooking potatoes in a huge automatic cooker for the hogs. I didn't mind that so much, although the hogs smelled terrible.

What I dreaded most was going to the barn twice a day with the grandmother and grandfather when they milked the cows. I had to hold onto their tails and, let me tell you, cows' tails can be very messy. I would hold on tight, but the cow would pull it out of my hand and in the blink of an eye, wrap her tail loaded with fresh manure around the head of one of the old people. I got into trouble, terrible trouble. I did a little bit better after a few weeks, but I never did know what to do with the manure on my hands afterward. At the end of the barn, manure was shoveled into a gutter, which had to be cleaned every day. That was another of my jobs.

It didn't take long for me to regret my decision because farm life didn't agree with me. It didn't agree with Ursel either. We stayed in a dormitory at night so we could commiserate with each other. We were city girls.

I didn't know how to build a fire. I didn't know how to milk cows. I didn't know how to chop wood. They gave me a little hatchet and sent me out to chop the kindling for the stove, but I never learned how to do it.

After six months, Mutti and Ursel's mother brought us home. Neither Ursel nor I could get through a whole year on the farm. We did not have what it took.

In a way, though, the farm experience was good for me because I learned to take care of myself. I became more self-reliant and less helpless.

When we returned from the farm in 1941, Ursel went to business school and I entered the government-controlled girls' school in Weimar. We had a little bit of horticulture education on Wednesday afternoons on how to plant and grow our own food in a little, bitty garden. This was not a bad idea.

At the beginning of the course, I gave the teacher my name.

"Macherauch, Macherauch. What was your father's Christian name?" she asked.

"Ernst," I replied.

"I can't believe it!" she said. "Your father, Ernst Macherauch, taught me in Erfurt. I had great respect for him."

So this teacher let me do whatever I wanted. I never planted a seed, but did lots of other things. In one class, when I climbed over the barbed wire fence to rescue a cat, I got hung up. They had to take me in and clean up the wounds on the back of my legs. I made a B in the class, not an A, and saved the life of a cat that disappeared again soon afterward.

We were also given lessons on how to cook and bake, but I always found someone else to do my work. It was like a game for me to try to get out of it. I didn't go to those lessons and I never learned the skills that were taught. I don't know why the teachers excused me.

I may have been the teacher's pet when I was 15. When we took sewing lessons, we had to make our own patterns and designs. I knew how to do that - no problem. We also had to make an apron and embroider it. I had material made up of little, bitty squares that should have been easy to embroider, but I couldn't stay on the lines. I showed it to the teacher, Fraeulein Tischer. She helped me a great deal.

When I told my mother, she said, "Why don't you ask Fraeulein Tischer to join us for Sunday dinner?"

Food was scarce at that time. My mother always felt sorry for single female teachers living by themselves.

"My mother would like you to come this Sunday and eat with us," I said in front of the whole class.

Fraeulein Tischer looked pleased and replied, "Fine! Fine! What is your mother having for dinner?"

I had been taught it was rude to ask what you would be fed when you were invited to someone's home so I thought fast and blurted out, "Roof rabbit."

Roof rabbit is slang for cat! The class howled with laugher. Fraeulein Tischer didn't catch on to what seemed so funny.

When my teacher came Sunday, Mutti served a rabbit that she gotten from Oma. I was scared that Fraeulein Tischer would tell my mother what I had called the meat.

Fraeulein Tischer was so grateful for the good meal that she finished my pattern for me and did a beautiful job. I made an A on the embroidery on the apron! She knew her business, but she was so nice we could wrap her around our little fingers!

One of my classmates came from a farm where they butchered their own hogs. She was so far behind in her homework that I did it for her so she could stay in our class. She paid me back by offering me two big slices of rye bread and a thick chunk of liverwurst sausage. It was a treat because food was becoming less plentiful in Germany as the war continued. My classmate later was forced to leave the school because she had failed too many courses.

Because I made good grades in my first year at the girls' school, Fraeulein Tischer came to visit my mother.

"Why don't you let Renate continue two more years at our school so she can become a teacher?" Fraeulein Tischer asked.

I was old enough to start thinking about my future. At that time, teenage girls who had finished school either were trained for an occupation or had to serve in the army in communications or administration or even work in a factory.

Mutti thanked her, saying she would consider the gracious offer. But she didn't want me to be a teacher. After Fraeulein Tischer left, she explained why.

"All the teachers I know are old maids and I do not want to see you end up an old maid," she said.

That idea didn't appeal to me either.

Later on, I learned the real reason Onkel Hans was very much against me attending that school. He resented that all my tests and papers were stamped with the swastikas. It was even the symbol on the school seal.

Again and again, I had to promise not to talk about what I heard discussed at home behind closed doors.

"We could lose everything, even our lives," Mutti warned me.

For once, I listened and began to understand more about what was happening in Nazi Germany.

After one year at the all girls' school, I had to have more education in order to support myself so I attended the summer semester at the Friedrich Schiller University at Jena. There, I took aptitude tests.

The United States declared war on Germany on December 8, 1941. Once the Americans got involved, many Germans said to one another, "That's the end of our war."

How could Hitler expect to go up against the whole world and win? We knew England maintained good relations with America, as well as

Canada and other countries. We had always heard that these countries were much, much bigger than Germany. We knew from our geography lessons at school that we were one little country.

But life went on.

The university sent a letter announcing that my test results indicated that I should be a nurse. I was instructed to report to pre-nursing school at Gera and dormitory Waldstrasse Number 1 on the 1st of October 1942. Bad Berka was located 50 kilometers northeast of Gera

"No," Mutti said. "That is a Third Reich school. You must go to the free nurses' school in Weimar."

My mother wanted me to be a blue nurse, a free nurse, but they were no longer allowed to accept students. I had to do what the Third Reich told me to do. My mother also wanted me to be a baby nurse, but that didn't work out either.

CHAPTER V

Pre-Nursing School in Gera

At the age of 16 in 1942, I entered the pre-nursing program at Gera. We received much better training than the blue nurses or the Red Cross nurses. (Nothing was too good for Germans enrolled in Hitler's pet programs.) Hitler and Nazi Germany saw to it that I paid nothing for my nursing schooling, not a dime.

Our food and clothing needs were taken care of by the Nazi government. Our toothpaste and toothbrushes, Nivea cream for our faces and Schwarzkopf shampoo - everything was provided to us free with the exception of shoes. We got 25 marks for pocket money every month that was deposited in a post office account.

Young girls like me entering the pre-nursing program were under very strict supervision. My mother and grandmother liked that. In fact, Mutti was relieved when she met my dormitory mother, Ruth. She was in her mid-30s, shorter than I was, and, oh boy, strict to no end. I don't think she was a Nazi because there were so few of them. She did what she had to do.

Almost every aspect of life in Germany was controlled by Hitler. He encouraged sports, music, so many things that were popular with youth. Some young people belonged to singing groups and dressed in their different regional costumes when they performed. Others participated in physical fitness activities. I didn't belong to those groups because Hitler kept me busy at pre-nursing school.

There were seven girls in my class. Even though we could not take one-step without supervision, I liked dormitory life. We lived on the second floor of the three-story building, which was located in a heavily wooded area about half a mile from the hospital. Student nurses, who were a notch above us, lived on the top floor of the dormitory.

We wore starched uniforms every day. I still have the cap and apron, although I don't remember the proper way to fold it. My pre-nursing uniform was a light brown light dress with a matching cap. Student nurses wore the same dresses, but the caps were white. Our dresses had to measure a certain length. We all wore swastikas on our chests. We looked very professional.

Our duties changed every six weeks. In the morning, we took care of our dormitory room and worked in the laundry or kitchen. The dormitory mother didn't start me in the laundry; she sent me to the kitchen, Mutti had tried to teach me how to cook, but I had paid no attention to her instructions. How I wished I had!

"Please God help me remember how Mutti did this and how she cooked that."

I dreamt about how I should prepare certain foods. Once everyone approved what I made, I was fine, happy to be doing the cooking. It wasn't very complicated because our diet consisted mainly of vegetables. Our dormitory mother bragged and bragged on me. I often made Mutti's potato dumplings. I had seen my mother shred potatoes for the dumplings and I recalled her telling me that she added a little water so the potatoes weren't dry. Mutti also said you had to keep the dumplings from turning dark. She told me that you had to cook them so long and then take them out when they were finished.

One night, the head nurse, who had been invited for supper, called and said she was running late because of a meeting and wouldn't be there at 7 o'clock. By the time she came, my dumplings were overcooked and smaller, but they still tasted good.

So in the kitchen, I never had to do dishes. I cooked and gave orders to the other girls on how to prepare the vegetables, things like that.

We had to do our own sewing, which we had learned in school. In the afternoons, we had four or five different classroom lessons - algebra, nutrition, music and general health care. I always made good grades. The courses were taught by our dormitory mother or doctors in training at the hospital.

Our dormitory mother would wear white gloves and check for dust even on the tops of the doors to the rooms. We had to open our lockers so she could see whether they were neat. I enjoyed all that. For the first time in my life, I had responsibility and I liked it very, very much.

But I still got into mischief. One evening, we were supposed go to a concert – Beethoven's Last Symphony. I was a 16-year-old girl with no interest in Beethoven. Three of us girls excused ourselves from the entertainment by saying we weren't feeling well.

After our dormitory mother and the other girls left for the concert, the three of us climbed over the stonewall surrounding our building and walked into town leaving the door of the dormitory unlocked so we could get back in. Our plan was to return before the dormitory mother and the rest of the girls, but we didn't make it. When we saw them walking back from the opera, we didn't dare pass them because the streetlights were still burning dimly and they would have seen us. When they went around a corner, we ran back to the dormitory by a different route as fast as we could. We crawled over the wall to find our dormitory mother waiting for us at the back door.

We were punished, of course. In those days, women mended their hose when they got holes instead of throwing them away. The dormitory mother gave us 15 pairs to darn that evening. We got through about 1 o'clock in the morning and then had a few hours of sleep.

Yes, we made our own entertainment in the dormitory. We prepared little skits and sometimes performed them three times on a Sunday afternoon for guests whom our dormitory mother invited. I was in favor of anything to break the monotony. I was never on the back row. I was always up front. I always volunteered.

We would stand in line outside every morning at 6 o'clock to do our exercises, winter or summer. It didn't matter if it was dark, cold, snowy, or wet. It didn't hurt us even when it was unpleasant. After we exercised, our dormitory mother read us the daily news from a newspaper produced by Nazi propaganda minister Joseph Goebbels. It always spoke in glowing terms about the Third Reich's efforts.

Near the girls' school that I attended in Weimar was the prominent clothing store of Sachs & Berlowitz. Mutti had shopped there many years before. I remember they sat me in a very tall chair in the office and a woman brought in different pieces of clothing to show us. That office and those tall chairs scared me. That's where Mutti bought my first wool dress called a Bleyle. The fabric scratched something terrible and it was too big for me, but I grew into it pretty fast. It surprised me one day to see that Sachs and Berlewitz had closed and its sign disappeared.

"Why did Sachs and Berlewitz close?" I asked.

"Because the owners are Jewish," Mutti told me.

During my first year in Gera, the Allied bombing raids began. One night, we peeked out of the upstairs windows and saw four Allied flares shining in our direction. It appeared that our dormitory could be the target, although it was actually the railroad station in town. When we heard the air raid siren, three of us girls decided we would not go down into the basement as we had been instructed. Instead, with great excitement we ran to a room on the third floor to get a birds' eye view of the bombing raid.

There were three beds in that upstairs room. When the bombs began falling, it didn't take long to frighten us so much that we each rolled up in a cover and crawled under a bed. I hid under the one closest by the window. Although our dormitory didn't suffer a lot of damage, the windows blew out. I will never forget the noise, the smell and the sound of breaking glass. The attack seemed to go on and on. When the bombing stopped, we crawled through the shards of glass covering the floor to the doorway and ran downstairs to safety. Had we not wrapped ourselves up in those bedcovers, we could have been killed. What were we thinking?

Our dormitory mother was furious. Our punishment was to stay in our room. We had to do our work, but nothing else for a week.

When we were grounded with nothing for us to do on Sunday afternoon, we got busy and thought of something. We decided to play our instruments to entertain German soldiers. One girl had an accordion, I had a guitar and another could sing. We dialed numbers on our telephone at random until we happened to reach a recovery center for German soldiers. The girl who sang got closest to the telephone receiver while we played in the background. This made a pleasant afternoon for all of us.

For a teenage girl like me, there wasn't too much for me to worry about because Gera didn't have a lot of industry. The Allied planes that flew overhead were often targeting Dresden, an industrialized city. We soon learned what the target might be depending on whether the bombers were flying high or low.

The year I was in pre-nursing school, I went home for Christmas even though I knew that my mother had gone to visit Onkel Hans, who was undergoing military training before being dispatched to the Eastern Front. Since there was no heat in the house and I couldn't make a fire, I went to stay with my girlfriend, Gerda, at her parents' house. She and I were together throughout my nursing training.

During much of the war, we read daily newspapers and heard radio programs, plus the mail service was very good. Mutti even sent me by mail a basket of gooseberries from our yard when they were in season. They arrived in perfect condition and I shared them with the other girls. We didn't get much fresh fruit.

We student nurses had little time to think about boys, but then again almost all the German boys were gone. They were already in the army or training in military schools.

However, during my stay on the farm in the country I had made a friend named Gerhard Spranger, who was 19, three years older than I was. After he was drafted, he asked to see me on his furlough. Gera, where I was taking my pre-nursing course, was not too far away.

Gerhard asked our dormitory mother for permission to go out with me. He was given strict orders to bring me back in two hours so I went with him from 3 to 5 o'clock. That would have suited my mother fine because she didn't want me to do anything wrong. Gerhard and I walked in the park and sat on a park bench holding hands. We stayed in close proximity to an air raid shelter in case the sirens went off and we had to take cover.

I enjoyed Gerhard's company. What a nice, polite young man he was.

When we got back to the dormitory, he told me, "I have talked to my parents and they have agreed. When the war is over and I come home, I will be old enough to marry you."

I treated him very ugly. "What makes you think I want to marry you? I may have someone else by then."

Of course, I hurt his feelings.

About four weeks later, his parents sent me a card announcing that Gerhard had been killed in action on the 28th of October 1943. I have always regretted my careless words the last time I saw him.

Another sad event occurred about that time. My baptismal sponsors, Dr. Dobers, and his wife, Charlotte, and their daughter, Camilla, lived near Bad Berka in the little village of Tannroda when I was a child. At the beginning of the war, the Nazi government transferred Dr. Dobers to Berlin. All three lost their lives during the bombing of Berlin in 1943. Mutti and I felt the loss because the Dobers had been so good to us and we had grown close to them over the years.

In our dormitory, my bed was right next to the door. Another girl, whose bed was around the corner, had a shortwave radio. Radios at that time were not plentiful. The news, which originated from a radio station in Luxembourg, was completely different from the news broadcasted every morning. It was not propaganda.

We listened to the shortwave radio whenever we got a chance. One girl stood guard outside the door to warn us if anyone was coming. After we heard the news of the day, we told the girl on guard what we heard. We were all very protective of that radio except for one member of our group.

"What you are doing is not right. We are not allowed to have a radio. I am going to report you," she threatened.

"You wouldn't dare," we told her. "If you do, we will make it very miserable for you here."

We meant it, too.

When the D-Day invasion of Normandy, France, took place on the 6th of June 1944, the news reached us right away. From our dormitory mother, we heard the Germans were winning. The Nazis bragged that they had pushed the Allies back from the Siegfried line, a long series of bunkers, tunnels and defense traps. When the announcers over the shortwave radio described the invasion, we heard the truth. The war was not going well for Germany.

When I say, "we" I mean the six of us girls who stuck together and discussed our situation. We weren't scared, though. We shrugged our shoulders and told one another, "Oh, well."

That had two meanings. One, "Germany has lost," and the second, "Will we be all right when Hitler eventually has to give up?"

As the Allied bombing picked up in intensity, the German people began to suffer more and more. Even with rationing, food was scarce; there were no shoes, no clothing, nothing. And the war kept coming closer. The Third Reich took 16-year-olds off the street. They didn't even know how to use a gun, but they were made to fight and so many of them were killed. Old men were sent to the front to fight. Everybody knew such desperate measures weren't going to work. What a sad situation.

While in pre-nursing school, I was allowed to visit my mother and often stayed overnight with Oma. First, she wanted to know about my training, but the conversation always got around to Hitler.

"He's crazy! The war is lost."

She couldn't understand why such terrible things were happening and why the war was allowed to drag on. Her viewpoint differed from what we were being told at school, but by then, I believed her. I told her what we had heard on the shortwave radio.

When I told my mother what Oma said, she was even more afraid. Oma would be jailed – or worse - if she talked like that to the wrong person.

In the fall of 1943, a caravan of about 30 to 40 German refugees came by on the road past our dormitory. We didn't ask these refugees where they came from, but we thought they were Volga or Black Sea Germans. German settlements stretched all the way to Russia on the River Volga, Oder River and the Black Sea until they were lost following World War I.

These poor, poor creatures carried the worries of the world on their shoulders and it showed on their faces. They were a pitiful sight, all so thin and dirty. In the group were mothers with babies, little children, young girls, young boys, old women and very old men. All the able-bodied older sons, husbands and fathers in those families were away fighting in the war. They traveled in a convoy of about 10 open farm wagons with wooden wheels and no covers over the tops. Their wagons were pulled by such pitiable animals; the majority were oxen, but they also had a few thin and tired horses. Along with all their possessions, they carried feed for their animals on those wagons. The refugees carried basic cooking utensils on their backs.

When the pathetic procession tried to climb the hill beside our dormitory, the women jumped down off the wagons. They were trying as best they could to lighten the load for the tired oxen and horses. The old people walked behind. I remember one mother handed the baby to a child on the wagon who was a little older. He reached out his arms and took the baby, even though he was still a child himself.

Our dormitory mother ordered us to serve the refugees something warm to drink and we were happy to do so. We were not accustomed to seeing people in such distress and felt compassion for them.

Since there were no plastic cups at that time, the travelers got their little cups off the wagons for us to fill. I ran back and forth to the kitchen to get the coffee. They were grateful for our kindness. We wished we could have done more.

The refugees were heading south toward Austria where there was less industry and more farming. They didn't want to go west because of the sustained bombing raids in that very industrialized region. Whatever happened to them I wonder?

After six months of pre-nursing training in Gera, I transferred to Weimar to help the county nurse for the next six months. We visited the homebound and dressed wounds. We also deloused schoolchildren and their families by pouring a certain solution on people's heads and massaging it into their hair; then they covered their heads with caps that resembled turbans for a certain length of time. After we took off the head coverings, we shampooed their hair. I loved visiting a lady who had a big sore on her head and watching the healing process over the course of my visits. I enjoyed that routine work very, very much.

I received word that for one week I would be assigned to private duty. I was to be picked up each day to help care for an old lady. How exciting for me!

On the first day, a car driven by one of Hitler's soldiers in uniform pulled up outside. I was a little scared, but I soon found out he wasn't so bad. His mother had broken her arm so I went every afternoon to wash the dishes and pick up fresh milk for her. Since there was no refrigeration, it had to be purchased fresh every day. After my chores were done, I walked back home. In fact, this soldier treated me well. I wasn't afraid of him, although I realized he was associated with Hitler. He wasn't hateful or mean like those violent, scary SS men who wore the ⚡ symbol on the sleeves of their uniforms. That lightning bolt insignia represented the special police that we feared.

When I was assigned to help care for newborn babies, I went to a very modern, fine home where a husband and wife of the older generation occupied the ground floor. The upper floor was occupied by a husband and wife of the younger generation from the same family. Both had new babies – mother and daughter. The baby upstairs was one week older than the baby downstairs was. The younger man was in the army and the older man was a porter at the Hotel Elephant in Weimar where Hitler liked to stay when he visited the city.

I couldn't wait to tell my mother about what I had seen.

"How is this possible?" I asked her. "Where do these people get the money to live in a beautiful new house like that? The younger guy is in the army and the older man is a porter. Those are not high paying jobs."

"This is what the Fuehrer promotes," she said. "Families get something like 20 marks when their first child is born and 30 marks when their second child is born. Parents get 40 marks for each additional child, which gives them almost enough money to live on from the children they produce. The more children people have, the less they have to work. They get a new house, too. That is Hitler's doing," she said. (A mark at that time was valued at about $1 U.S., if I remember correctly.)

"That is not right," Mutti added.

I agreed. This was wrong.

The last two months that I worked for the county nurse in Weimar,

I helped a young woman 10 years older than I named Frau Anneliese Benz. She had polio and a new baby. I would go to see her each morning and little Thomas would be waiting for me to take him out of his crib. I would feed and bathe him and see what assistance his mother needed. She was all alone because her husband, Willie, had been drafted as a pilot in the German army. On weekends when I went home to see Mutti, I sometimes took Thomas along with me. He was a joy and Frau Benz was very grateful. She recovered from polio, but walked with a limp and used a cane even though she was not an old woman. ☽

CHAPTER VI
....

No More "Heil Hitler"

O n the 1st of October 1944, when I started student nursing, we were allowed to work with patients. Half the hospital, which was large and modern for its time, was filled with regular citizens and the other half with military personnel. For six weeks, I worked on the surgical floor where there were men, military on one side and civilians on the other. We had to stand by to care for the wounded that came to us in Red Cross ambulances.

The head nurse recognized me because I had cooked for her when she came to visit our dormitory mother. She always called me "Little One," although I was the tallest of all the girls.

From that time on, I had no opportunity to listen to the shortwave radio. Whenever there was an air raid siren, we had to drop whatever we were doing and report to the hospital to move patients into the basement. We no longer took shelter in the basement of the dormitory.

Before the Allies bombed, they would shoot off flares from their planes. This was new to us because when we were pre-nursing students, we always had to be in by dark. The Allies most often targeted industry and railroad stations. Sometimes bombs fell elsewhere by accident. Accidents like that happen in war. The Gera train station was bombed because from that central location, trains went off in four different directions.

After an air raid siren went off in November 1944, my friend, Gerda, and I had instructions to check and make sure all the patients had been taken to the basement. She was a step ahead of me when we heard a deafening crash. I called to Gerda, but she couldn't hear me so I dived in a patients' room for safety. When I heard her call my name, I ventured back into the hallway long enough to catch her by the dress and pull her in with me. A bomb had damaged our hospital's west wing in that attack.

Because the air raids had become so frequent, there were no more lessons. We student nurses had to work full time with hospital patients. We reported to the hospital after every air raid and some weeks rarely returned to sleep in our dormitory beds. Gerda and I would take turns hiding for an hour or two to take a nap in a bathtub on the upper level. We always made sure that we knew where the other one was in case the head nurse called us.

Red Cross workers were always the first ones on the scene to treat the wounded. It had been set up as a permanent relief agency for humanitarian aid in times of war. The rules of war in the Geneva Convention recognized the neutrality of the agency, allowing it to provide aid in a war zone. Two Red Cross helpers on each floor of the hospital emptied bedpans and changed linens. They were not skilled, but good at what they did. The Red Cross was a positive force, a positive influence.

The hospital was overflowed with civilians wounded in air raids and soldiers injured from the fighting on the Front. Nearby schools or large buildings taken over by the government served as hospitals for stabilized patients. In the basement of the hospital was a long hallway with rooms off both sides. Huge heating ducts ran down the middle of the ceiling, which made it look a little ominous even though it was clean.

We saw a lot of patients crying and screaming in pain. I remember staying with one soldier who had been given medication, but was still suffering. I talked to him, trying to calm and ease his mind.

When the door swung open there stood a doctor.

"Nurse," he barked, "come over here!'

The patient whom I had been talking to put out his hand and grabbed my uniform.

"Don't leave me, please don't leave me," he cried out.

He tried to hold me back, but I had to do as I was told.

Although I was only a student nurse, the doctor expected me to help him with surgery. He took off his white smock and handed it to me. I put it on and tied it in the back. I wasn't prepared to go into surgery. I had no mask, but I did my best.

I was working in the burn unit with the head nurse when an opera singer was brought in. She had been burned over more than 40 percent of her body when the hall where she was performing was bombed. Only her face remained untouched. The rest of her body was grotesque beyond description. She died in a few days. I had seen soldiers who had been burned, but they were already patched up by the time they reached the hospital.

I witnessed the disgust that certain doctors could not hide when they gave first aid to very young soldiers. Sometimes these physicians would find an excuse to pack a boy-soldier in cold towels and send him to a hospital that treated infectious diseases when he had come in with only a sore throat. Other boy-soldiers who had a finger or a hand wound were put in casts and transferred to sanitariums for the duration of the war. The doctors wrote on their records that the boy-soldiers were unfit to fight. At least they saved some lives that way.

I tried very hard to please the head nurse and the doctors, but on one occasion, an intern made me feel very foolish. It came over the loud speaker in the hospital that such-and-such a group was to report to the basement.

He saw me in the hallway and said, "That means you."

So I went to the room where the lesson was being delivered, an autopsy was being conducted. My stomach lurched and the intern, who made me attend the demonstration, chuckled. I turned around and rushed out of the room.

Overall, I found my student nursing very interesting. For example, when blood was needed, the patient had to be connected to the donor. The blood was not drained and stored as it is now. We turned a mechanical wheel by hand to transfer the blood. Although very primitive, the procedure worked.

From the 1st of October 1944 until we were released in March of 1945, I was not able to go home to Bad Berka because we were needed at the hospital. However, I wrote letters to Mutti every week to tell her what I was doing. She would write back to me and I learned that my hometown hadn't been bombed, although Weimar had. I also wrote to see how Oma was doing and she wrote back that she was doing fine and getting enough to eat.

My mother and grandmother's biggest concern was whether I got enough to eat. I reassured them that we student nurses were always fed enough. We never had much meat, but lots of vegetables. Our meals were simple. With our milk and a hot cereal called Griesbrei for breakfast, we were allowed two tablespoons of white sugar. We also drank coffee made from barley, and for dinner, soups and stews were served. In the evening, we had one piece of rye bread. I still like the smell of rye bread.

The morning after every air raid, we student nurses received extra rations - smoked eel. I ate smoked eel until I couldn't eat it anymore, but I knew my mother could use it. I packaged it up in some brown paper and sent it to her in the mail. There was no protective plastic available and the postal carrier complained that the oil from the eel soaked through the paper. Mutti was so glad to get it that I kept on sending it and the post office kept on delivering it. Suffice to say, I have never eaten smoked eel since the war.

Mutti was a little short of food, but she had a garden. Besides potatoes, she grew peas, carrots, cabbage and lots of rutabagas. She also had enough room in the yard for some chickens. Part of our old woodshed became a chicken house with a little run. Although I was a student nurse and didn't live with Mutti, she could count me – not for the ration cards – but for hens. Each German civilian was allowed to have one and a half hens. Mutti was allowed to have three because of me, but she was breaking the rules. She had four chickens. When she got word that the local police were going around Bad Berka counting chickens, she put one of the hens in a gunnysack and kept it in the basement out of sight for three days. My mother was not afraid of the local police; she didn't want the fourth chicken to be taken away from her.

I had to deliver medication to two wounded English officers who were prisoners in the hospital. As student nurses, we had been instructed to say, "Heil Hitler," whenever we went into a patient's room. When I closed the door behind me with my medication tray, I was scared because these men were English – Germany's enemies. I was also afraid that I wouldn't do the right thing in carrying out my duties.

I grasped my tray and murmured, "Heil Hitler."

They started laughing and responded, "Heil Hitler." They were making fun of me. I must not have personified the enemy they were fighting.

By then, I didn't buy into the Nazi propaganda. One day when I carried a tray of medication in little cups down the hallway, I met the chief surgeon.

"Heil Hitler," he said, raising his right arm straight out in the Nazi salute we had come to despise.

"Heil Hitler," I mumbled, rushing by, my eyes downcast. I knew I was in trouble when he called me into his office.

He threatened me, but I managed to talk my way out of it.

I told him I was afraid of tipping the loaded medicine tray. I don't know whether he believed me, but he gave me the benefit of the doubt. After that incident, whenever I saw that doctor coming toward me, I either ducked into a room or turned around and headed back in the same direction that I had come.

Because I was so young, the German soldiers liked to tease me. One day when I delivered medicine, one of those young guys in the ward got down on his knees in front of his buddies and proposed. They were laughing hard when I fled the room. I asked the head nurse if someone else could be assigned to that ward. I didn't want to go back there again.

After Christmas 1944, nobody cared if we said "Heil Hitler" or not. We didn't dare say "Heil Hitler" to our wounded German soldiers. They had had it with Hitler as well.

I asked the head nurse about a young girl in a private room one day.

"Why is she getting special treatment instead of being put in the general ward with other patients? And why is her incision in a different place than others who have had appendectomies?"

"The surgery was performed under one of Hitler's programs," she told me with disgust. The girl had been sterilized because someone in her family had been reported to have mental problems."

This sterilization program supposedly weeded out so-called genetic defects from the German gene pool. How disgusting. The thought of Hitler's highhandedness made me sick. It made me dislike the Nazis even more, if that was possible. Around that time, I began hearing more about his "master race," and felt relief that I wasn't blonde and blue eyed.

By then, most of the hospital staff didn't mind speaking out about the Nazis. The bomb plot in July 1944, in which senior German army officers attempted to kill Hitler and end the war before our country was destroyed, had failed. Although not the first attempt on Hitler's life, that one came closest to being successful.

"Who or what can stop Hitler?" we wondered aloud to each other.

I received a letter from the government saying I must volunteer in case of a fire. Since I had no firefighting training and my skills were needed at the hospital, the directive was greeted by laughter. The head nurse and other workers at the hospital shook their heads. It didn't make sense.

Toward the end of March 1945, Gerda and I both received a letter from the government informing us we must volunteer for military office work or communication duties. When we presented these instructions to our head nurse, she told us to go to Weimar to seek a written exemption because student nurses were much in demand. We were already doing our part for the war effort.

Although the train ride from Gera to Weimar usually took about an hour, Gerda and I spent three hours making that trip. The train had to stop and all of us passengers get off every time an air raid siren sounded. The engineer found underpasses for shelter where we waited out the air raids because the streets were built above the train tracks in many places.

It was afternoon when we finally made it to Weimar and the city was topsy-turvy with confusion. When we got to the street where the National Socialist Party headquarters was located, a big bonfire burned on the lawn in front of the building. We couldn't imagine what was going on. Halfway up the stairs to the second floor, we met the lady whom we were supposed to see. We stopped her and told her who we were and why we had come.

Half-listening, she shoved a huge armload of paperwork into our arms and said, "Take this out and put it on the burn pile. Then come back and see me."

We did as we were told. Back upstairs in her office she said, "The Americans are on the other side of Erfurt. What you burned are your records. Children, you don't have to do anything now. Try to go home if you can."

We began to hear artillery firing in the distance. The fighting was that close? This was news to us. We had been warned that when the Allies took over a city, they fired shells over an open field as a warning to announce their arrival. We were very frightened.

The lady had told us to go home, but we were reluctant to leave our belongings at the nursing school in Gera because we had no way of replacing them. We went to the little station to catch the train to Bad Berka about 4 or 5 o'clock in the afternoon. The train schedules were very unpredictable because of the frequent bombing raids and we had to wait. Finally, when the Bad Berka train began to board, we changed our minds.

"Let's go back to Gera," I said to Gerda and she agreed.

"Yes," she said. "Let's go and pick up our clothes. Maybe we'll still have a chance to get home."

After we watched the Bad Berka train pull away with mixed feelings, we walked to the other station to catch the Gera train. But no more trains were scheduled so we had no way of getting back that night.

It was getting dark so what were we to do? Across from the train station in a little park was a tiny bench next to the sidewalk. We sat down with our little knapsacks beside us, clinging to each other in fear when darkness fell. It was eerily quiet. I must have fallen asleep because I was awakened by a pounding noise on the road nearby.

"What is that?" I whispered.

"It sounds likes footsteps," Gerda whispered back.

I walked to the end of the sidewalk. Although there were no streetlights, I could make out German soldiers marching by in the night.

I got close enough to ask one, "Where are you going?"

"Away from here. The Americans are on the other side of Erfurt," he said, never breaking his stride.

That's what the government lady had told us earlier in the day.

The next morning, Gerda and I took the first train that ran back to Gera at about 7 or 8 o'clock. When we got to Gera around noon, we ran as fast as we could to our dormitory.

We opened the front door and shouted at the top of our lungs, "The Americans are here! The Americans are here!"

Our dormitory mother came out of her office, scowling. "The Americans are not here," she informed us.

She was wrong, but we didn't dare argue. We told her that in Weimar we had been told to go home. We'd just returned to the dormitory to get our clothes, but she didn't want to hear it.

"Do you know what you are saying? You could be charged with treason against Germany and punished with death. Go to your room and stay there."

In our dormitory, we hastily packed our knapsacks in case we were allowed to go home and then sat on our beds looking at each other. We had had nothing to eat all day, but we were so fearful that we had no appetite.

About three hours later, there was a knock on the door and we were told to come downstairs. We left our knapsacks on our beds. Our dormitory mother did not mention any punishment for Gerda and me. Instead, she spoke gently, telling us to be more careful and sensible.

"Come to the meeting tonight when the head nurse will instruct us on what to do. That's all for now," she said. We went back to our room and waited, still very scared.

That night the head nurse told all of the pre-nursing and nursing students that the Americans were fast approaching central Germany. Of course, Gerda and I already knew that.

"Those of you who are adults report to the hospital. You have work to do. Those of you who are under 21, go home if you can," she said.

It was night already and there were no more trains so we went upstairs and crawled into our beds. Would we ever return to our dormitory after that night?

In the morning, we put our knapsacks on our backs and walked to the station to board a train home to Bad Berka. We took the swastika pins off our uniforms and threw Hitler's symbol away. It was the last week of March 1945.

When a siren blew, we had to get off the train and take shelter under a bridge until the air raid was over. At Oberweimar, the last station before Weimar, there was another air raid, but it didn't last longer than a half hour. ☽

CHAPTER VII

Bombs, Blood, Bewilderment

When we got to Weimar, we were stunned to learn that both the train we had decided against taking the day before and the Bad Berka Station had been bombed. We felt sick to our stomachs. We had come that close to being killed. Thank goodness we had gone back to Gera.

We were told the train would get as close as it could to Bad Berka that day. Some people got off in Legefeld. The station was crowded and we could hear the artillery fire in the distance. There were a total of eight or 10 cars in the whole train. Gerda, an old lady and I were the only occupants in the third car behind the locomotive. Gerda and I amused each other by commenting that if we sat near the front of the train we'd get home sooner. We were that anxious.

As the train started to roll again, we heard the unmistakable rumble of fighter planes, one behind the other, making a beeline for us. When they got close, they were flying so low we could see the faces of the pilots firing the machineguns. It was horrible, terrifying.

Machinegun fire hit the locomotive first. When the train shuddered to a stop, our car was situated between a telephone post, a wooded area and a building. People in other cars started scrambling off and running for shelter. The three of us crawled under the seats of this old-time railcar for protection, although my backside stuck out. I hung onto my knapsack with my teddy bear in it and I prayed.

"God, please protect me."

Because I had trouble getting my shoulders under the low seat, I was a little afraid I would be shot in the backside. Despite my fear, I thought hard. Where could we go? Then I remembered that my father's cousin, Tante Hercht, managed that train station and the building had a basement.

The planes were coming at us in groups of three, hammering the train and everything in the vicinity. The lone vehicle on the road, a van on the street with a huge Red Cross symbol on its side exploded with a deafening roar. The so-called Red Cross vehicle had been filled with explosives. How had the Americans known it was not a real ambulance?

After the second group of fighters passed over, I called to Gerda,

"Let's get out of here."

The old lady, who had hidden under the bench across from me, leaned over, patted my cheeks and pleaded with me. "Don't leave me, Fraeulein. Please, don't leave me."

We waited until after the third pass of the planes. Then Gerda and I rushed out of the railcar for the nearby building, taking the old lady with us. We just made it into the station when we heard more planes. We crawled into a huge freestanding empty wooden wardrobe in a room with one window. Squashed in together like sardines, we waited and waited for the incessant racket to stop. We couldn't quite close the door and when a shell burst through the glass, we were too frightened to scream. After a while, there was silence. We pushed open the door a little and peered out before we came out to join the people walking upstairs from the basement.

My father's cousin, who didn't seem surprised to see me, made the observation, "I guess it's safe to come out now."

Blood was everywhere outside. Dead bodies, including those of the engineer and the conductor in their uniforms, were all over the street. People were crying and screaming. The train had been demolished except for the third car in which we had been riding.

We turned our back on the terrible sight and focused on our predicament. How were Gerda and I to get home to Bad Berka now? We still had about six kilometers to travel. Not wanting to chance going down the streets, we decided to try walking through the woods.

On the road, we saw a group of about 25 or 30 men in filthy striped uniforms marching, more dead than alive. There was so little life left in them, they were so beaten up, that they looked to neither the left nor right. They plodded along, with just enough energy to put one foot in front of the other. These were Allied prisoners taken from a prisoner of war camp before the Russians or Americans could arrive to liberate them. The guards with these men looked half-dead themselves, although they wore different clothes. The men were all so pitiful they frightened and unnerved us. As 18-year-old nurses at the hospital, we had seen a lot of misery among the wounded soldiers and we had witnessed death, but somehow, this seemed worse. Heartless.

Gerda and I ran the other way. Still scared to death, we made our way across a little meadow to a road where an old flatbed truck loaded with German civilians stopped and picked us up. When we thought we heard more fighter planes coming, the truck stopped and we all jumped off and ran into the woods to hide. When the planes were gone, we got back on the truck and it went on.

We were so happy when we got home to Bad Berka. We hugged before we parted. She went to her home and I went the back way to my mother's house.

I opened the back door and called, "Mutti!"

There was no answer. I couldn't think where my mother could be.

"Mutti! Where are you?" I called, but there still was no answer.

I opened the kitchen door to find her sitting in the wicker chair next to the window, her face as white as the dead people I had seen on the street.

"Mutti!" I cried. I was very scared again. "What's wrong?"

She turned her head and blinked, her eyes trying to focus on mine. Then she whispered, "You are alive!"

"Sure, I am alive," I said, puzzled.

"You are alive!" she repeated. "You are alive!"

"Yes, I am alive and I have come home," I told her.

We hugged and hugged until she pulled away from me limp with relief, and looked at me again.

"Oh," she said touching my face. "You have camouflaged yourself."

At first, I didn't understand what she meant, but then it dawned on me that when the old lady on the train touched my face, she had smeared coal soot all over it. That was the "camouflage" that my mother saw.

Two days before I came home, Mutti had received word that the Bad Berka train and station had both been demolished. Nothing but the concrete foundation was left. A survivor who had seen me at the train station earlier in the day told my mother that she thought I had been on the train when it had been bombed. When I had arrived home, Mutti had been seated at the kitchen table gathering her courage to go to the morgue and identify my remains.

I didn't know it then, but I had come home six weeks before the official end of the war. During the last month of the war, there were no German vehicles to be seen anywhere. All travel was on foot.

Because our house was big enough, Mutti was informed by the authorities that she must give up some of her rooms to refugees. A girl named Helga moved into my old room. The office in which she worked had been transferred from Berlin to our hometown the year before. Her boss lived elsewhere in Bad Berka. We also had three teachers living in our house. A Jewish lady had one room and the two other women occupied one big bedroom and a small room that used to be my father's office. Later on, Helga's boss came to live with us so the three of us – Helga, Mutti and I – bedded down on the living room floor every night because there were not enough beds to go around. When the air raid sirens went off, we took cover in the basement.

After I was sent home from the nursing school, normal communications in Germany broke down and mail was no longer delivered. Mutti still had telephone service, but so few people had telephones it wasn't very helpful.

German civilians passed along news and information, as well as rumors, by word-of-mouth. My mother was afraid to listen to the Nazi propaganda on the radio that still broadcasted that the Germans were winning the war. We knew it wasn't true.

Mutti went to buy what little food she could before daybreak.

The night before the Americans moved in, cannon fire roared from one side of our little city to the other. It reminded Gerda and me of what we had heard in Weimar. No houses were hit. It was a frightening warning that the Americans were moving in.

⋆⋅∶⋅◉⋅∶⋅⋆

We blamed everything on Hitler who shot himself the 30th of April 1945 in his Berlin bunker. How did his suicide make me feel? My first response was regret rather than disbelief. Too bad Hitler got off so easy. In the end, he was a coward. What a shame he wasn't caught and taken to trial to face his crimes against humanity.

After Hitler's death, the war in Germany ground on and on. During the final weeks of fighting, United States army forces pushed beyond the agreed upon boundaries for the future zones of occupation. It was during this period that American army troops occupied my mother's home twice with no forewarning.

One day there was a knock at the door. An American soldier speaking German told my mother we had 15 minutes to gather our personal belongings and leave. Her house was being requisitioned for use by the U.S. Army.

We grabbed some clothes and what little food we had and went to stay with my stepfather's sister. Tante Elly still lived in a small apartment above the office at the health spa that my stepfather had operated before the war. Although she had an extra bed for Mutti, Helga and I slept on a small sofa. In order to fit, we curled up in the fetal position, on opposite ends, which wasn't very comfortable. The slanted ceiling was so low that Mutti had to stoop over to get in and out of bed. The other people who were living in my mother's house were provided with rooms elsewhere in Bad Berka.

During the war, that complex had been utilized by the German army as a recovery center for soldiers. By the time we sought refuge there, the former spa was occupied by the Americans and served the same purpose.

Tante Elly didn't even like letting us look out the windows to see what the Americans looked like, but we caught glimpses of them through cracks in the closed drapes. In our mind's eye, we pictured them like the cowboys in those old Wild West movies, but we were impressed. They were well dressed, clean-shaven and better fed than we were. They looked very civilized.

Hitler had decreed years before that every German household should have a copy of his book, *Mein Kampf*, which translates in English to "my struggle" or "my battle." Hitler's book, a combination of autobiography and political ideology, exposed his brutal racist philosophy. When my mother heard the Americans were close by, she buried important documents that bore the Nazi swastika in glass jars, along with her copy of *Mein Kampf* in the chicken yard. She feared that the Americans would be angry if they saw the book in her house. This caused me a great deal of consternation because I needed some of those documents so she had to dig them back up. However, she never bothered with *Mein Kampf*. It rotted right where it was buried.

We had virtually no Negro population in Germany. The sole Negro I knew of was a porter at the Hotel Elephant in Weimar. We were a little scared of those American soldiers who had a different skin color, but Oma set us straight.

"Don't be afraid," she told us. "They are human beings just like us."

She was alone when the first American soldiers arrived in her village. She answered a knock on her door to find American Negro soldiers with guns. They told her they were checking every house looking for Nazi soldiers who might be hiding out. She said she reached out and took one of the soldier's hands and looked at the inside of his palm. It was white. We were surprised that she would do that. When we realized we didn't have to fear the Negro Americans, she said, "I told you so."

If the local police asked Oma a question she didn't think was any of their business, she told them so. She put up with nothing she considered "nonsense."

After the U.S. Army took over our house the first time, they stayed a week. They emptied the larger rooms by piling the furniture all the way to the top of the nine-foot ceilings in the smaller rooms. They brought all their own equipment, furniture and supplies.

When the Americans departed on a Sunday morning, the GIs went around official orders to leave us as much packaged food such as crackers, as they could. Before we could get back to the house, however, some boys broke in and stole the provisions. We were not surprised because everybody was so hungry. Mutti found that only the pillows on the sofa and the guitar I had played during my pre-nursing school days had gone missing. Everything else was the same as she had left it.

Before the end of the war, Frau Benz, whose small son I had looked after in Weimar, sent a message with our mail carrier. He told me, "Frau Benz says if you don't have other plans, please come and stay with her in Weimar. She is expecting her second child and needs help."

"Well, it's not so far away," Mutti said. "It will give you something to do."

So I took my little knapsack and walked to Weimar alongside the mail carrier, a man in a navy blue uniform who was respected by all who knew him. No trains were running out of Bad Berka because the train station had been bombed.

After the war ended, the Allies agreed to separate our country west of the border between Germany and Poland, the Oder-Neisse line, into four occupation zones: American, British, French and Russian.

The American zone included the provinces of Bavaria and Hessen in southern Germany and the northern parts of the present-day German state of Baden-Wuerttemberg. The ports of Bremen on the lower Weser River and Bremerhaven at the Weser estuary of the North Sea were also placed under American control. Under U. S. General Dwight D. Eisenhower, the Allied troops were to begin helping rebuild Germany's infrastructure and reestablish civilian government.

That is the short and sweet description delivered to the outside world. For us German civilians, the occupation was not so cut and dried. Hitler's name was not mentioned any more, but our country and its people could not escape his legacy. As Oma had predicted, we would pay for Hitler's heinous actions behind the gates of places like Buchenwald prison.

According to the website http://en.wikipedia.org/wiki/Buchenwald_ concentration_camp, between April 1938 and April 1945, some 238,380 people of various nationalities including 350 western Allied prisoners of war were incarcerated in Buchenwald. One estimate places the number of deaths in Buchenwald at 56,000. While it was called a concentration camp rather than an extermination camp, an extraordinary number of deaths occurred there. Many inmates died because of human experimentation or fell victim to arbitrary acts of cruelty perpetrated by the SS guards. Other prisoners were murdered.

Appalled by the atrocities carried out in Buchenwald by Hitler and his Nazis, the liberating American soldiers loaded up on flatbed trucks German civilians who lived nearby, including women, and took them to see the camp of horrors. ى

CHAPTER VIII

A Nation Crushed and Defeated

On the day World War II ended, the 7th of May 1945, I was staying with Frau Benz in Weimar. When we heard a knock at the door, she looked through the peephole and saw two American soldiers who appeared to be officers.

The propaganda about the troops that would be coming through was frightening. The Allies, which of course included the Americans, had defeated Germany. They had won the war and Germany had lost. The Americans were among our conquerors. We understood this post-war period would be a strict army-type occupation. We were the civilians of a beaten, crushed nation.

Frau Benz pushed me back out of sight behind her because she didn't know what they wanted before she opened the door a crack. We were both surprised when one of the American officers addressed her in German.

"Your husband, Willie Benz, is safe," he said. "He has been taken prisoner at the Nohra Airfield at Weimar. Once he has been interrogated, we will bring him home."

Frau Benz started trembling. Although the American had spoken to her in German, she responded in English, "Thank you! Thank you!"

We watched the two Americans turn and head back to their jeep parked on the street. We watched them drive away. We looked at each other in disbelief. We were speechless. Could it be true? Frau Benz couldn't wait to find out!

About 4 o'clock that afternoon, we heard an automobile approaching. There weren't many vehicles on the road at that time so it got our attention. Peeking around the edge of the curtain, we saw an American jeep pull to a stop outside. Seated next to the American GI driver was Frau Benz's husband, still wearing the uniform of a German pilot.

What a joyful reunion for Herr and Frau Benz and little Thomas. It seemed like a miracle. How could something like that happen? The story fascinated me.

Many years before, the parents of Herr Benz had taken him to New

York to visit members of their family. He and his family liked the United States so much that they stayed and Herr Benz went to school in New York from the third grade through high school. The family planned to become American citizens, but there was no rush.

In 1938, Herr Benz and his parents returned to Germany to visit his grandmother. Their timing could not have been worse. When the war started, they were not allowed to return to America. Of course, a fine young man like Herr Benz was drafted into the service. He became a pilot and a German officer.

When the war ended, Herr Benz had been stationed at a German air base in Czechoslovakia. He made up his mind to join the Americans where his sympathies had always been. He jumped in his plane and flew away before anyone could stop him. When he landed in Weimar, he held up a white flag and presented his remarkable story in perfect American English. Not only did the Americans believe him, they recognized he could serve a useful purpose during the occupation. The next morning, a jeep picked up Herr Benz and that day he started work for the Americans as a translator.

Mutti answered a knock on the door one day to find an American soldier who told her in polite broken German that she would have to leave her home for a second time. The Americans were going to occupy the house again. He stayed and waited while Mutti, Helga and I packed up, giving her time to go down into the basement where she stored potatoes. Food was so scarce that she didn't want to leave them. The others living in my mother's house also had to leave. Frau Biesi moved into a confiscated Nazi home, along with Herr Luederitz and Sigrid.

A young GI from New York, who was a guard, told Mutti about his grandparents who lived in Dresden, although he had been instructed not to talk to German civilians. He feared for their lives because the city had been bombed repeatedly by the Allies.

During the six-week occupation by the American Corps of Engineers, a big mess tent for their troops was erected in our garden, destroying much of our beautiful yard and the gooseberry bushes. However, all the trees survived. An American GI, who had been warned not to offer food to German civilians, gathered bacon grease left over from the preparation of the soldiers' food. He poured it in a green army tin and left it for us in our woodshed. We had to eat it there, too, so no one else would see us. We put it on our bread and were glad of it because there was so little food by that time. We had no idea how he got it. There were only certain days he could do that.

As a child, I never experienced hunger, but during and after the war I knew lots of people who went hungry. Tante Frieda literally starved to death. She would eat the food she received with her ration cards in two days. After she filled up, she had nothing to eat the rest of the week. She would stop by our house and my mother would always give her something even though Mutti didn't have much. It must not have been enough because when Tante Frieda got ill, it didn't take long before she weakened and died.

Mothers with little children faced the worst deprivation because there wasn't enough milk or nourishing food to go around. Those who lived in the city had it the hardest. Those who lived in the country had more of an opportunity to trade something for additional milk from a farm.

About a week before the Americans moved on for the second time, the same guard told Mutti, "We are soon going to vacate your house. I don't know where we are being sent."

The young American soldier was devastated. He thought it would be unlikely that he would have a chance to check on his grandparents in Dresden. Mutti couldn't help herself. She embraced him as if her were her own son.

War is so cruel.

The Americans had been ordered to leave our region of Germany to make way for the Russians to take over. We had prayed that the Americans would take all of Germany, but that didn't happen. Why wouldn't they let the Americans go all the way through? Why, we all wondered?

We German civilians had no use for the Russians. We were very upset about their impending arrival. No one had anything good to say about them. It was a political deal – a bad deal - from our perspective.

The news of the pending Russian arrival was devastating to my mother. She was 48 years of age and all alone. In 1944, my stepfather had been pulled out of the military office where he worked for the Nazi government and put in a uniform so he could fight on the Eastern Front. We had not heard from him in a while. Mutti didn't know what to do and truthfully, there wasn't much she could do.

When the Americans pulled out, they left behind what we would classify as trash. In post-World War II Germany, any scraps were precious so we rushed to the house before anyone could break in and steal them as they had done earlier. Some plates contained good-sized pieces of soap and others were filled with cigarette butts. We dumped out kitchen matches and gathered up enough cigarette butts to fill two of the boxes half-full. They measured about five inches long and three inches wide.

Then we discovered that more cigarette butts filled the gutter on the second floor outside the upstairs window. Helga and I tied ropes around our waists and crawled out on the steep roof to gather them. Mutti watched us, praying for our safety. By the time we finished, we had almost three full boxes of cigarette butts. We took them to the bakery and traded each box for a long, four-pound loaf of bread over a period of several weeks. These were such a wonderful treat.

I would stay with Frau Benz for a few days and then I would go back and stay with Mutti. Frau Benz liked having me around for company during the day and I was able to help her with Thomas. Because of her polio, she found it difficult to carry him downstairs. They lived in a small one-bedroom apartment and I slept on the little sofa in the living-dining-kitchenette area.

There hadn't been any regular mail delivery for months, making communication between relatives difficult. We were fortunate to live within walking distance of Peppi and were able to send word back and forth with people we knew. Peppi had taken up residence in the Macherauch family home six kilometers away in Legefeld with her daughter, Kristel. She managed what had been my father's berry farm. Peppi was forewarned that she would have to vacate the big house because it would belong to "the people."

"I have a message from your sister, Elisabeth," a mutual friend told me. "In case she has to leave the Macherauch house, she wants you to take some silverware and a painting for safekeeping. It should be given to your half-brother, Wilhelm."

We had had no contact with Wilhelm for six years. We didn't know where in Canada he lived, but Peppi hoped that someday we would be reunited. She tried to gather everything possible including Wilhelm's silverware and a painting of the family's home in Legefeld before she left the house. It had been painted by Peppi's husband, Erich.

Peppi and Kristel got a two-room apartment in Weimar where she took a government job, as she was instructed. Her husband, Erich, who had been drafted in 1944 at the age of 40, still was listed as missing in action. (He would never return.) Since I would do anything to please my Peppi, I agreed to her request. I put Wilhelm's silverware and painting in my satchel.

About two weeks after the war ended, the bright yellow mail carrier's vehicle called the Postauto started running again in Bad Berka and the surrounding area. This bus not only carried the mail, but 12 passengers, as well.

On the last Friday of June 1945, Herr Benz sent word that the Russians would soon be taking over the Weimar area so he planned to come with an American army truck and driver to move his family and their belongings. They wanted me to come with them. I knew I had to work somewhere to be eligible for ration cards so I went home and told Mutti about the offer.

"I don't want you to go," she said, "but we have heard such awful stories about the Russians that you will be better off with Herr and Frau Benz. If they don't need you any more, promise me you will go back to school to finish your education."

I promised Mutti that I would respect her wishes. I also promised her that I would come back home and check on her when I could. Then I took my knapsack and left to travel with the Benz family when they moved on Sunday.

I threw the satchel containing the silverware and painting on the back of the truck and kept my knapsack in my lap. We drove on the autobahn because parts of it had not been bombed. When we passed an American military vehicle headed toward us, the driver blew his horn and motioned at us.

"What do you think is wrong?" asked Herr Benz. When we looked behind us, in the road we saw a dark bundle. The satchel containing Wilhelm's silverware and painting had bounced off the load so we backed up so I could retrieve it.

Herr Benz crossed the Werra River, which flowed near Eschwege but not through the city. After stopping several times for information, we were told we had been assigned a room in a three-story apartment building that backed up to the train station in Eschwege. We climbed the stairs to the second floor and rang the doorbell of an apartment, as we had been instructed to do. The lady, who answered the door, had no extra room as far as she was concerned, but had been told to make room for us. People had no choice; they did what they were told. The woman's husband had been drafted and she had two little children.

Some men helped Herr Benz unload some of the furniture from the truck. In our room were two single beds and a baby bed for Thomas, as well as a small table and chairs. The room had a balcony, but no bathroom. There was a toilet and washbasin in the hall.

On the 2nd of July 1945, the borders closed between East Germany and West Germany with the Werra River as the official dividing line. We had gotten out of East Germany with little time to spare. However, Mutti was still home in Bad Berka in the zone controlled by the Russians.

When the Russians arrived in Bad Berka about a week after the Americans left, Mutti told me they looked hungry and unkempt - pitiful.

After I left home, 20-year-old Helga must have been a great comfort to Mutti. She seemed relieved to be under Mutti's protection because her parents had been killed in an air raid and she had no other family. Mutti didn't let Helga out of her sight. They stayed locked up in the house a lot. Some of my school friends were raped by the Russians. The Russian soldiers were mean and hateful. Always on their guard, German civilians kept their doors locked to keep the Russians out as best they could. The Russian occupation seemed very, very primitive and very, very disorganized. The Russians didn't even seem civilized. For example, when they vacated an apartment they had occupied, they ripped the faucets out of the walls instead of taking them apart.

During the occupation of the Russian zone, there were informers like there had been in Nazi Germany. There always seem to be people who are willing to turn in others to further their own interests. The power must have made them feel important, plus they got extra money so they could live well.

Wearing civilian clothes, Herr Benz left with the American military government and we were left alone. We had no idea where he would be sent and neither did he. Communication was still next to impossible. No mail delivery. No newspapers. No radio. No news. We waited and waited.

Frau Benz's new baby, Uwe, was born on the 6th of August 1945. He was little and he cried non-stop. He needed more milk because Frau Benz wasn't getting enough food to nurse him well. She got ration stamps for milk, Thomas got ration stamps for milk and the baby got stamps for milk, but it still wasn't enough. We also fed the cereal Griesbrei to the children.

We went to pick up our rations well before dark because of the strict curfew. We often took the children with us because they needed a little bit of fresh air and sunshine. The American soldiers would be on one side of the street and me, a young girl, with Frau Benz and the children would be on the other. Of course, they made remarks, which I ignored.

Frau Benz got upset with me.

"You could at least show them a friendly face," she said.

My mother had warned me earlier, "When men get really friendly, watch out. They want something. They can't be trusted." Is there any wonder I was scared to death of the American soldiers?

"No, I don't want to smile," I said.

One day, Frau Benz nodded to an American soldier standing alone on the street and he took that as a signal to follow us home. She invited him upstairs to our room, although he knew, and we knew, that the American soldiers were not supposed to enter German homes. At first, he talked to Frau Benz. After a little bit, he started talking to me. Frau Benz seemed very happy. I didn't like him at all. I felt sick.

"I have to go to the bathroom," I said, my heart pounding.

When I left the room, I ran and hid upstairs in the attic, leaving the door open a crack so I could hear when he left. That happened twice.

I prayed and prayed that nothing bad would happen to me. I knew Mutti would be upset if she thought Frau Benz was encouraging me to be friends with an American soldier in exchange for food. I thought of Peppi, too. If Peppi had been there, I knew I would have been safe, but neither Mutti nor Peppi were around.

September came with no communication from Herr Benz.

We attempted to do laundry for American soldiers in exchange for food and cigarettes so we could buy more food on the black market, but the basement laundry room seemed to be occupied seven days a week by other German civilians who had the same idea. We tried doing laundry as late as we could in the evening, but then we had a problem drying the clothes. We would have to hang them on a line in the attic. Although Frau Benz took in the laundry, I did most of the work, but I didn't mind.

The food we got with our ration cards on Saturday mornings was supposed to last for the whole week. The meat would be gone by Sunday even though we tried to stretch it by making soups. Through our ration cards, we got whatever vegetables were in season such as carrots and beets. The quantity was not plentiful but enough. Frau Benz traded or bartered the cigarettes we had for soap and meat and butter. We had enough bread to last us a week if we ate two slices per person per day, the same way Mutti had rationed it. This heavy dark brown bread tasted good. There were shortages on items such as toilet paper. What we could get was very rough.

I am not proud of it, but I stole food from our neighbor in the next apartment because I couldn't watch Thomas and the baby starve. The neighbor's pantry next to our kitchen had been walled only partway to the ceiling. Frau Benz helped me climb over the top so I could open the door from the inside. I took a jar of hazelnut butter for the children from the pantry. We did what we needed to do to get by. ☽

CHAPTER IX

Same Moon, Same Stars

In September 1945, Frau Benz told me, "Renate, I am tired of living like this. I've got to find out where my husband's unit went."

One of the American soldiers, who had his laundry done upstairs, provided her with a lead. Although he had no definite information, he thought Herr Benz's unit might be in Stuttgart.

On the 11th of September, Frau Benz left me with the two children and went to search for her husband. Early in the evening several days later, I put the children down for their naps and went to mail a letter I had written to my mother. Even though mail was still not moving between West Germany and East Germany, I wrote to Mutti every week with the hope that one day she would get one of my letters.

When I returned, I stopped to chat with a young woman named Marga Neumann, who lived upstairs with her parents. We were standing talking in the doorway when two American soldiers walked by and glanced our way.

We remarked to one another, "They may be going to town to look for girls."

I had once been pretty naïve, but I now realized that these American soldiers liked to find willing girlfriends. At the end of the street, the Americans stopped, turned around and walked back toward us. It was the 14th of September 1945.

The one with blue eyes asked in German, "Why do you stand there?"

Shaking, I reached in my pocket before replying, "What is wrong? I have my ID card. See?"

"There's nothing wrong," he answered. "This is my first day in Germany and I want to practice my German."

He seemed a little awkward, but nice awkward, not too sure of himself. The other guy never spoke a word. The soldier who was a little taller than me did all the talking.

"Where are you from?" I asked, attempting to make conversation as I tried to stop shaking.

"Texas," he said.

When we studied geography in school, I had learned about the Gulf of Mexico and dreamed of seeing it someday. That's where I recalled seeing Texas on a map.

"Is Texas near the Gulf of Mexico?" I asked.

"Yes, you're right," he said. He seemed pleased.

"You speak German well," I told him, although he used some words differently and his sentence structure wasn't quite right.

He didn't really seem to know what to say so he proceeded to tell me about himself. He lived on a farm in Texas and his family spoke only German at home, although he had learned to speak English in school. His great-grandparents emigrated from Germany to Texas, except one grandmother, who came to America as a small child. He had been drafted by the American government. He hadn't volunteered to join the army. He had been in England before being transferred to Germany for the reconstruction effort.

I found him quite interesting, but I had little experience with men, let alone American soldiers. Was I curious? Yes.

Because of the strict curfew, at about 6 o'clock, Marga and I turned to go in.

Before we closed the door, the guy from Texas asked, "Can I talk to you again?"

I had no idea why he wanted to talk to me. I felt a little tongue-tied in his presence.

"I don't know," I said. "I don't think so."

"Well," he said, "I would like to."

When I went to mail another letter the following evening, I wondered if I might see him. Sure enough, he came striding down the street toward me, alone this time. Frau Benz still wasn't home.

So we talked. He told me his age and told me more about his life in Texas.

"We have the same moon and stars in Texas as you have in Germany," he said. I found that very interesting to me because I thought Texas was close to the South Pole.

After we talked some more, he asked, "Can I see you again? I want to practice my German."

"I don't think so," I replied.

"Why not?" he demanded.

"I am married and have six children," I told him.

"Where is your husband?" he asked.

"He's a prisoner of war," I replied.

"I don't believe you," he said. "Can I talk to you again?"

"I don't think so," I said. My answer was not a definite "yes" or a definite "no."

The next night, Frau Benz still wasn't home.

On the night of the 16th of September, this American guy turned up again.

I thought to myself, "He is nice to talk to. He isn't like some of the American soldiers who are so pushy. He seems honest. I like him."

"I don't believe you have six children," he told me.

"No, you're right, I don't," I replied. "I have two children. If you don't believe me, come upstairs and meet them."

"I'm not allowed to," he said, "but, yeah, let me see these two children of yours for myself."

At the top of the stairs, a thin strip of light shining under the apartment door shocked me. I had left the apartment in darkness. When I opened the door, Frau Benz was sitting at the table eating. I hadn't seen her return because she slipped in the back door that faced the train station.

"Oh my goodness," I thought to myself. "Now this American guy is going to find out I don't have any children."

When Frau Benz saw a young man wearing an American soldier's uniform behind me, she didn't hesitate.

"Come in, please come in," she said in English, smiling and making him feel welcome.

He took off his cap, shook her hand and introduced himself.

"My name is Harvey Meiners. I am pleased to meet you," he replied in German.

It pleased me to see how respectful and well brought up he appeared to be. Frau Benz was all smiles.

Although Harvey could soon tell that Thomas and the baby were not my children, he didn't say anything about my lies. Thomas welcomed Harvey warmly so he lifted the little boy out of bed and played with him for a little while.

Before he left, Harvey asked me, "Can I see you again?"

Frau Benz answered for me. "Sure!" she said.

I shrugged my shoulders and the color must have risen in my cheeks. What would Harvey think? I knew what Frau Benz thought. We had heard that American soldiers always brought a big sack of groceries when they came to visit civilians in their private living quarters. That's what she wanted.

So Harvey got into the habit of stopping by every night.

On the night of my 19th birthday, the 1st of October 1945, Harvey asked, "Can you sew, Renate?"

"Of course," I said. "Why do you ask?"

"I have been promoted to staff sergeant and I'd like you to put the new stripes on my uniform."

"I'll be happy to," I told him. While we sat and talked some more, I stitched.

When I finished and handed the jacket back to him, he said, "Whatever you find in the pockets is yours."

A bar of Camay soap was in one pocket. What a thrill! The only thing available at that time was floating soap, which wasn't real soap at all. I don't know what it was. How I treasured that bar of wonderful soap!

"Thank you, Harvey, thank you so much. This is the best birthday present I have ever had!"

He smiled, pleased his small gift had brought me so much pleasure.

The other pocket contained a package of cigarettes.

Frau Benz said, "Give me those cigarettes and I'll trade them for food."

And she did.

From then on, I mended whatever clothing Harvey had that needed attention. I didn't mind.

Harvey often brought something for Thomas even though the gift sometimes wasn't suitable for a child. It was his way. Sometimes he came with cigarettes, sometimes candy, but it was never enough for Frau Benz. She didn't seem to care that every month Harvey sent money home to his parents.

"That Harvey, he's a stingy GI," she told me.

I resented her saying that, but I let it go.

The first time I invited Harvey, that lonely American soldier, to eat with us, I fried potatoes in peanut butter. There was no bread to go with the peanut butter and potatoes. That's all we had. Harvey said he hadn't had fried potatoes since he left home. The children liked them and Harvey said he did, too, but I didn't.

The American soldiers were still warned not to fraternize with German civilians, but that didn't bother Harvey.

"I speak German and I know my way around," he always said.

Most of the American soldiers couldn't speak German, of course. They seemed to pick up a few words and phrases, some of which were not too good.

When I told Mutti about Harvey, she asked, "What religion is he?" When I said, "Lutheran," she relaxed.

So Harvey and I often stood outside the house where I lived with Frau Benz and we talked. Those were our dates because there were no restaurants, no entertainment, nothing. We always were mindful of the strict curfew, but one Friday night two or three weeks later, we had bad luck. An American military policeman on patrol with an MP band around his arm drove by and saw us. He stopped.

"What are you doing?" he demanded.

"We are talking," we told him. (Marga was there, too.)

"You are breaking the curfew. Come with me," he pointed to Marga and me.

Harvey couldn't talk the MP out of detaining us and Marga and I didn't dare argue. During the occupation, the word of the American army was law. The MPs had to keep order and enforce the rules.

The MP drove us to the police station in his jeep.

How terrible! Frightened, we kept looking at each other as if to say, "What are we doing here? What are they going to do with us?"

We didn't know what to expect.

It was unbelieveable. I, Renate Macherauch, was being detained at the police station like a common criminal. What would this disgrace do to my family's good name? What would my father have thought? I made up my mind that nobody would find out. Even though I fingered my identification card in my pocket, I decided to save my family from that embarrassment.

As it got darker, the MPs brought in more and more people. At last, we were taken to a vacant schoolhouse set up as a dormitory with 10 other women. Marga and I didn't want to have anything to do with the others so we ran and found a bed together, but we didn't sleep well.

In the morning, we went downstairs where a German civilian recorded our names and addresses. I again gave my name as Lieselotte Saenger. Marga gave her real name because her mother knew she had been picked up.

In the early afternoon, the same civilian worker came back to the crowded room where we waited and leaned over to talk to me.

"Where are you from?" he asked.

"My hometown is Bad Berka, but I live here in Eschwege now," I told him.

"Is your name Lieselotte Saenger? Now tell me the truth. We punish those who lie to us," he said. Seeing my fear, he reiterated, "Tell me your real name."

I started to cry and through my tears told him my real name. Then he wasn't so stern. He told me his wife came from Bad Berka. His first girlfriend had been a friend of my half-brother Wilhelm's. He invited me to visit him and his wife at their home. That made me feel better, but it didn't lessen my guilt at the thought of having a police record.

"Please, please, don't notify my mother," I begged him. "She will be mortified."

"Don't worry about it. You didn't do anything wrong," he said.

What I hadn't counted on was Harvey getting word to Frau Benz that Marga and I had been picked up. When Frau Benz came to check on me, they told her no one by that name was being held, but she insisted there must be some mistake. She knew the military police had picked me up the night before.

Before Marga and I were released, blood samples were taken to check us for venereal disease. Social diseases were running rampant with so much unprotected, casual sex between American soldiers and German women.

It was such a relief to get home to Frau Benz, Thomas and the baby, and of course, to see Harvey again.

Frau Benz had located her husband when she went to Stuttgart so she was waiting to join him. On the 15th of October, he told her to cancel the rental agreement with the lady who owned the house.

Frau Benz was so glad to get out of that icy cold room. The authorities had denied her request for coal. Why? Perhaps she didn't have enough money to buy it on the black market. Frau Benz and the baby moved in with Frau Johannes on the third floor, while Thomas and I stayed with Marga's parents for a few days. We slept in Marga's bed because she was not home at the time. As soon as a civilian vehicle became available, Frau Benz and the children were moving to Stuttgart where the family would be reunited.

Frau Benz said, "Renate, come with us and help me. I expect we will be doing lots of entertaining and you can look after the children."

By that time, Harvey had been transferred. He had no idea where he would be stationed. I was neither surprised nor disappointed. Wartime friendships were temporary, especially between German civilians and American soldiers. Harvey's departure left me feeling sad, though, and unsure of what I should do.

Perhaps I could get a position as a helper in a pharmacy scheduled to start in January 1946, although who knew if that would happen. Perhaps nursing school would start again in the new year? Again, no one knew.

What I did know was I had had no word from my mother for four months. Was she alive or dead? I had no winter clothes and the weather was getting cooler and cooler. I had nothing to eat. I had no place to live. I made up my mind that I would go home to Bad Berka. That meant I had to make an illegal crossing from American-controlled West Germany to Russian-controlled East Germany.

Marga did laundry for Harvey's friend, a soldier, who promised Harvey he would look out for me. He went in and out of the apartment upstairs and often sat in the kitchen visiting. Sometimes I talked to him.

"How can I cross the Werra River?" I asked him.

"I know of somebody who might take you," he said.

I had no food so I traded the last package of cigarettes that Harvey had given me for a big jar of pickled herring and half a pound of butter. I wanted to take the jar of pickled herring home to my mother. The bread and butter Marga's parents had given me were soon gone. All I had left in my knapsack was my jar of pickled herring.

I dressed in a wool pleated grey and red skirt and a top that I made from part of my shirt. I had knitted a short sleeve sweater for the front of it and, of course, I wore a coat. Though it was wartime, I was a young woman. When I knew I looked nice, I felt better about myself and the chaotic world in which I lived.

The soldier dropped me off near the border at a guesthouse that was not open for business, similar to what my mother used to run. By then, my pickled herring had been eaten.

"Goodbye and good luck," he said. "The milkman who delivers between East Germany and West Germany will be coming along soon. He will put your knapsack in one of his big milk cans and sneak it across the border. He will also give you an address where you can pick it up after you cross the border."

I went inside and the old couple who lived there fed me well. They were so kind. They tried to talk me out of attempting to cross the border.

"No, no, you must not try to go to East Germany," the woman said, very agitated. "The Russians killed three people the other day. Why must you do this?"

"I have to. I have to," I told her. I was frightened, but very determined.

When the milkman knocked at the door, I gave him my knapsack as the American soldier had instructed me to do. A short, dark haired older man, he seemed a caring, fatherly type of person. He reassured me that my knapsack would be safe with him.

I stayed with the old couple for three days trying to figure out what to do. How far away was the border? I couldn't see it so when night came, I took a walk to the river bridge. I noticed the steep bank and the little American guardhouse, a temporary looking structure, next to the bridge.

Looking around, I thought to myself, "This is so open. No wonder the Russians shot those people. I can't cross in the daytime, but at night? Yes, perhaps."

I made up my mind to try in the evening of the third day. Since I had nothing to carry, my hands were free. I made my way to the bridge in a roundabout way and crawled down the embankment to wait for the right moment. When it got dark, a light came on in the little guard hut on my side of the river. I could see the soldiers sitting around the table laughing and talking.

"Help, help," I cried out to the Americans using the English I had learned from my tutor. "Help me get back to the Russian side where I came from."

I didn't speak any Russian so I knew if they challenged me, I was in trouble.

When the bright lights of a jeep hit me in the face, I was blinded. I froze in my tracks. I wasn't afraid I would be shot because the Americans didn't do that. I thought they would send me back, though. The jeep stopped at the guard hut and blew its horn. I could hear them talking.

"Hello, here's the mail," an American GI said.

"Okay, thanks."

When the jeep turned around, the lights shone right on me again. I remained standing like a statue. Then the jeep left and the Americans went back into their guardhouse and closed the door. They didn't even seem to notice me.

I ran halfway across to the bridge and put my hands up over my head before I shouted in German, "Help, help." When no one responded, I ran to the end of the bridge where the Russian guardhouse door stood wide open. The checkpoint was deserted. What a relief! Later, I heard that no guards were on duty that night because they were striking for more food.

I made my way to meet the milkman at his home, where they

served me a super-duper lunch of bread and homemade sausage. It had been a long time since I could eat as much food as I wanted. It tasted wonderful! The milkman and his wife gave me a beautiful bed to sleep in. Their kindness brought a lump to my throat. Both the old people at the guesthouse and this couple treated me as loving grandparents would treat their treasured grandchild. They had arranged for the mail carrier to take me to the next train station and even made me a sandwich to take along for a snack. I got my knapsack back, too.

No money changed hands. So many caring, kind German civilians helped others out of the goodness of their hearts. I was fortunate to have encountered a number of them.

When I met the mail carrier the next day, he said, "Come with me."

By the time we left the village, six of us were walking with him to Treffurt, which took about an hour. We went along the Werra River, sometimes walking in the riverbed where we got our shoes a little wet. When we got to the top of the riverbank, there stood Russian guards. They asked for our identification cards, but I didn't have an identification card.

At first, I played dumb.

"What have I done with my ID? I just had it out. Perhaps it is in my change purse? No, it is not there. Is it in my knapsack? No, it is not there either."

When the others showed their ID, I started to panic. Harvey had once given me a little piece of paper with a postage stamp on it. It looked so interesting I had put it in my pocket. Out of desperation, I waved that little piece of paper and the guards waved us through.

I had to wait for the Bad Berka train a little bit before I made it home to my mother's open arms. Although I was weak with exhaustion, we were so happy to see each other.

"What would you like to eat?" Mutti asked.

My favorite meal had always been fresh carrots and peas with butter, salted potatoes and meatballs, so that's what I requested.

"I can fix you the peas, the carrots and the potatoes," she said, "But there's no meat and no butter for the potatoes."

Mutti still hadn't heard from my stepfather. Was he a prisoner of war or had he been killed? She offered me a pair of shoes that belonged to Onkel Hans. They were a little bit too large, but they worked. I could still wear my old high top shoes that I had gotten on my 12th birthday, although they were pretty worn out by the end of 1945.

I needed to register with the police so I could get my ration cards because Mutti didn't have enough extra food. I hesitated because I realized that once I did so the chances of getting out of East Germany again were slim.

I told Mutti what I had been doing. I explained that Frau Benz had taken the children to Stuttgart where her husband had transferred with the American military government. I told her I had sent Wilhelm's silverware and painting with them. These keepsakes were safe with that family.

I had a message from Herr and Frau Benz to deliver to two ladies who worked in a certain store in Weimar. Since the trains were still not running, I rode an old timey bus. I was shocked at the condition of the beautiful old city. Weimar still was in shambles. It was as if the bombing had just occurred.

After delivering the message, one of the women asked, "How did you cross the border?"

I explained. Then she asked, "Are you going back?"

"I want to," I said, "but I don't know how."

"We are going in two weeks and we'll take you with us," she said. "We have enough cigarettes to pay off the Russian guards. Our plan will work. We have done it once already. We will cross at Treffurt."

"I have nothing to pay off the Russian guards," I told them.

"Don't worry," the woman told me again. "We'll take care of it."

Since I had crossed into East Germany at Treffurt, the surroundings were familiar to me. I liked the idea, but decided to go home and talk to Mutti.

"I don't mind if you go back to work for Frau Benz," she said, "but I want you to finish your education. I want you to be a nurse."

I didn't tell my mother that Frau Benz had sent word that she would welcome me in Stuttgart because they gave big parties to entertain American officers. The family occupied a big house with servants and Herr Benz had his own chauffeur.

I didn't tell my mother that I had big misgivings about what would be expected of me if I went there to live. What about all those soldiers who were far from home in an occupied country? How would I be expected to provide amusement for these male guests?

These young American men liked the girls and the girls had no protectors. Their brothers and fathers were either dead or prisoners of war. The Americans were not bad, but they were idle and liked having a good time. Alcohol flowed freely. If a girl looked at a soldier with a friendly face - a smile - he assumed she was a willing partner.

Once, an American soldier followed me home although I had definitely not given him a friendly face. In fact, I had made a point of ignoring him, but he was so drunk his sour breath reeked of stale beer. He grabbed me when I went to unlock my door. When I could see he wasn't going to let me go, I took my key ring and jabbed him with all strength on the shoulder. He swore and I ran.

When I met the two ladies who had offered to take me back to West Germany, I wore my overcoat. I offered to carry another big coat for one of them over my arm because I had merely a knapsack for luggage. The three of us traveled to Treffurt.

At the train station, one of the ladies left to see the Russian guards at the border. When she came back in a little over an hour, she didn't say much. They put another light coat over my coat, and then a coat with a fur lining over that.

"These coats are so heavy, I don't know if I can walk all the way to the border," I complained.

"You have to," the women told me. "We'll go slowly."

We waited until dark before we started walking across the meadow. It seemed like a long way. I thought we'd never get to the other side. Then we saw three Russian guards. One of the women went ahead and greeted them in Russian, while the other said to me, "You stay right here."

She put a wool scarf around me and loaded me up with so much more clothes, I could hardly move, which was part of their plan. The women told the Russians that grandma (me) was limping. By the time we went across the bridge, I truly did limp. The guards weren't interested. They waved us on.

On the other side, the women took those heavy coats off me. Then we walked what seemed like a long way again before we came to the American guardhouse. We stood right in front of the guardhouse window so they could see us in the light. In English, I called out, "Hello, hello, hello," but they paid no attention to us so we went through.

We had made it back to West Germany safely.

The ladies had the address of a person who could take us on to Eschwege so we knocked on the door of the first house we came to, but nobody answered. They had no way of knowing who we were or what we wanted. So we kept trying, going door to door until we found the right person. A few more private vehicles were on the roads by that time.

When I got back to Eschwege, Harvey's friend, George Wockenfuss, had two messages for me. George, who was also Marga's boyfriend, had received a letter from Harvey, who was stationed at Fuerstenfeldbruck Air Base near Munich. He and a few other enlisted men and hundreds of prisoners of war were rebuilding the airfield and hangars that had been destroyed in Allied bombing raids.

Harvey told George to encourage me to come to Munich if I should come back. He had found a job there for me in the American post office, as well as a place to stay. Harvey's message didn't excite me.

"I don't know," I told George. "I still have some of my belongings in Stuttgart."

George could read my indecision.

"You know, Harvey is a good guy, an honest guy," he said. "He is not taking advantage of you. I think he is serious about you. He cares about you. He has a job and a place for you to stay. You can't ask for anything more than that."

George also had a message for me from Herr and Frau Benz. They wanted me to come back to Stuttgart.

"I don't know," I told George again. He must have thought how ungrateful I seemed. Without his help, Harvey and I would never have found each other again and I would not have been able to keep in touch with Herr and Frau Benz either.

I couldn't make up my mind right away so I stayed in Eschwege for a couple more days with Herr and Frau Neumann. I went again to check on when I could start work in the pharmacy, but it still was not scheduled to open until January.

What a terrible time this was for all German young people because we could remember better times. I was so discouraged. Some days it seemed like my life was over before it had begun.

"Go to Munich and the home of Frau Schmidt at Maisacherstrasse Number 4," George advised. "Harvey has made arrangements for you to live there."

Still turned upside down and inside out from the war, normal transportation was a long way from being restored to its pre-war efficiency. That's why it took me two days to get to Stuttgart, a trip that would have taken only hours years before.

That meant I had to spend the night in the horribly dirty and dimly lit Frankfurt train station. It was almost bursting with displaced persons and German soldiers. I found it hard to find room to set my knapsack down where I could sit on it. A woman I talked to suggested that I go downstairs and find a bunk to sleep in. She promised to watch my knapsack. The basement was filled with people milling around the huge space broken up by row upon row of bunks. Finally, I found an empty upper bunk and climbed into it. Then I felt an urgent tap on my shoulder.

"Lady, that's my bunk. Go somewhere else."

Discouraged and a little claustrophobic, I went back upstairs to find the woman who had my knapsack. I couldn't even sit down on it then because the station was even more overcrowded than before. A German soldier returning home from the war occupied the space where I had planted my feet earlier.

He asked where I was from and where I was going. Sensing that I was not too enthusiastic about traveling to Stuttgart, he said, "Come home with me. My family has a big enough house. You will be welcome there."

I think he meant it in a nice way so I thanked him, telling him I had to go to Stuttgart to pick up my belongings.

The next day, I made it to the Benz home. They were so glad to see me that they greeted me with big hugs. Herr and Frau Benz repeated their offer, "Stay and look after the children and help us with the parties we host for American officers."

I was still hesitant so I told them, "I don't know. I have a job promised to me at the American post office in Fuerstenfeldbruck and I have a place to stay. I am supposed to start next week."

Frau Benz bristled.

"Has this got something to do with that guy, that cheapskate American GI who kept coming to our apartment in Eschwege?"

I didn't like the sarcasm in her voice, but I didn't want an altercation so I lied to her. "No, it has nothing to do with him."

I thought to myself, Harvey had never asked me for anything, which is more than could be said for most of the other GIs I had met.

In the beautiful Stuttgart villa where the Benz family lived, I shared a huge room with three-year-old Thomas. The baby slept next door. Thomas begged me to stay and that made me sad.

"Thomas, maybe I will come back," I said. That seemed to satisfy the little boy. I asked Herr and Frau Benz if I could leave the satchel with the silverware and painting for Wilhelm with them. After they agreed, I ironed my few pieces of clothes. Despite the war, we still ironed our clothes! At that point, I had to wash my underwear every day. At the beginning of the war, I had four changes, but they were worn out. When I was a child, my mother told me that my underwear always had to be clean and so I kept it clean.

Then I said goodbye to the Benz family, caught a train to the last station before Munich, and walked to Fuerstenfeldbruck. I reasoned that if things didn't work out, I could always leave and come back to live with Herr and Frau Benz in Stuttgart. When I arrived in Munich, I found the address that George had given me. I knocked on the door of a first floor apartment. When the door opened, I introduced myself.

"Renate, we have been waiting for you," Frau Schmidt said. "Come in, come in!" She had the same surname as Oma, although they were not related.

I had been raised in the central part of Germany and now I was in Bavaria. Frau Schmidt spoke German, but her dialect was so different from mine that I found her difficult to understand. She introduced me to her two boys and told me her husband was still missing in the action like so many others. I was to sleep in the living room-kitchen area. The boys and their mother slept in the bedroom. I was very grateful to have a safe roof over my head, but the apartment was so small, I had no privacy. I took sponge baths at night after the lights were turned out. Nevertheless, how very, very generous Frau Schmidt was to let me live there.

"Harvey comes every day to ask if we have heard from you," Frau Schmidt told me. "He should be here in about an hour. Why don't you hide and surprise him?"

Years before, my Peppi and I would make a loud sound to call each other.

"Ewit, ewit," we would say. Harvey had been amused when I told him the story. That night when Harvey arrived, I hid in the bedroom.

"Have you heard from Renate?" he asked Frau Schmidt.

"No, sorry," she told him.

"Why is she not coming? Maybe she will never come," he said. I could tell he had missed me.

That's when I called out, "Ewit, ewit."

Harvey knew who it was! He was so happy to see me. I was happy to see him, too. Everything was good between us!

I started working at the military post office the next day. Then I went to the police station to register for my ration cards.

Those of us who were working in the post office were very lucky to be able to eat in the mess hall. By the middle of November 1945, the post office began receiving early Christmas packages for the American soldiers. Some parcels that hadn't been packed well were falling apart when they were delivered. Every day, we had loose chocolate, cookies and other treats spread around the room where we sorted mail. Everything that came in that couldn't be delivered was put in a sack and divided between those of us who worked there.

I had it made! I had a good place to stay and as much as I could eat at work. What an impressive array of food. I had never seen that much meat in my life! However, we weren't allowed to take any food home in a sack so we had to use our ingenuity.

In those days, women's stockings were held up by elastic garter belts. We figured out how to stash some food from the broken packages in the tops of our stockings. Although walking with the extra bulk presented a challenge, I was able to take food home to share with the Schmidt family. They were very grateful because there still wasn't enough rationed food to eat.

At work, we sat down for our meals after the soldiers had gone back to their duties. Every day outside the post office area, old and hungry men who worked at the airfield, lined up. They would stand at the fence holding out empty tin plates, hoping we would share our leftovers. Some American soldiers treated them ugly, but others scraped the food they weren't going to eat on those plates. It was going to be thrown away anyway. I, too, felt sorry for these old men.

I watched and soon picked up on how best to share my leftovers. I filled my plate with more food than I wanted and pushed some of it aside. I didn't even touch it. Then I would go outside and scraped that leftover portion off my plate and onto theirs. The old men were very grateful. So many German civilians still were hungry.

In December, I took Harvey for his first sleigh ride. He got so scared, he dug his heels into the snow and we almost ran into some trees. We laughed and laughed, although there was precious little warmth that holiday season. At the Christmas service, the church was cold and cheerless with no decorations and no music. Only the pastor's sermon spoke of Christmas. How I longed for the warmth and happiness I recalled from the Christmas observances of my childhood.

My gift from Harvey that first Christmas was a pair of boots! They were my first new boots since I turned 12. My old ones were worn very thin. I had also been wearing Onkel Hans' hand-me-downs, but they were clumsy looking and a little too big. I felt badly that I had no gift for Harvey, but I had no money to buy anything on the black market.

Our dates were very simple. Often, Harvey and I sat on a park bench, snuggled together in the cold with only our love to keep us warm.

In a letter from Mutti, I learned that the Red Cross had notified her that my stepfather was alive and being held as a prisoner of war in Dachau prison, about 50 kilometers from where I lived.

Through the Red Cross, my mother wrote to my stepfather and told him where I was living and that I had an American boyfriend who spoke German. Although it took a long time to be delivered, the mail went through. It seemed strange that she couldn't write to me because I lived in the Western Zone and she lived in the Eastern Zone, but she could write to my stepfather, a prisoner of war in the Western Zone.

Any information contained in mail going to the Western Zone, no matter how innocent, was censored if it did not reflect well on conditions in the Eastern Zone. For example, if I wrote that I had eaten a good breakfast of bacon and eggs, the letter wouldn't go through. If I wrote saying I was able to purchase a pair of new shoes that information was censored, as well. Why the Russians cared, I don't know.

On the morning of the 8th of January 1946, I was describing a beautiful dream I had had the previous night about clear, clear water to Frau Schmidt. It had been very soothing and made me feel so good. I looked out the window and there was Harvey. How nice! He had stopped by with some rolls for our breakfast, but he couldn't stay.

Harvey had to go to work so he went out, jumped in his jeep and made a U-turn, oblivious to the big American army truck stopped in the street across from the Schmidt's house and a man who had gotten out of it.

"Harvey almost ran over that poor guy!" I turned to tell Frau Schmidt.

When I turned back to look out the window, I noticed the man from the truck coming toward our house. He looked a little familiar to me. Then I did a double take.

The man was my stepfather dressed in his German army uniform! What was he doing here? I was thrilled to see him and couldn't wait to hear his explanation.

His account amazed me. It seemed unbelieveable. He said since the Americans always took some prisoners along when they went to get supplies for the camp, he had volunteered to go. He told his captors that his stepdaughter lived in Fuerstenfeldbruck, a city along their route. The GIs dropped him off for a visit with the understanding that they would pick him up on the way back to the camp in a couple of hours.

Onkel Hans was an American prisoner and they took him along on the truck and let him off? Then they would come back for him a couple of hours later? How could this be? This was all new to me.

Onkel Hans had been captured by the Americans in the northern part of Italy. His outfit was supposed to be guarding something, but he didn't know what, in 1944. They remained isolated in the forest so long that they had no idea that the war was over because communication with the outside world was non-existent. When American troops found them, they tried to defend themselves.

A German-speaking American soldier told them, "The war is over, don't fight any more. But we're going to take you prisoner."

Onkel Hans and the other German soldiers were relieved.

"When did the war end?" they asked. They hadn't wanted to fight Hitler's war in the first place.

The prisoners were transported to the closest prison, Dachau, where they could not have been treated better. What a difference a few short months American command had made at that dreadful place. In fact, it is difficult to comprehend.

On the 29th of April 1945 when the Allies liberated Dachau, they described it as "a gruesome spectacle of wholesale bestiality and barbarism." It is estimated that over 200,000 prisoners from more than 30 countries were held there under appalling conditions and subjected to hideous, inhumane treatment. About two-thirds of these were political prisoners and nearly one-third was Jews. The world will never know the exact number of people who were interned or lost their lives there.

Now a little more than eight months later, the Americans were bending over backwards to treat their German prisoners well. No doubt, they had seen far too much of the Third Reich's atrocious wickedness. It speaks well of the Allies that they didn't retaliate against poor German soldiers like my stepfather who had been forced to follow Hitler and his Nazis.

How wonderful that my stepfather was alive and well! The two-hour visit went fast. At the appointed time, the American army truck pulled up across the street again, waiting to take Onkel Hans back to Dachau.

When Harvey arrived the next day, I said, "You almost ran over that poor guy getting out of that big army truck yesterday."

"Yes," Harvey said, "I didn't see him. I'm so glad I didn't hit him."

"Me too," I said. "That was my stepfather!"

Harvey could hardly grasp my news. Since the Americans allowed their prisoners of war at Dachau to have visitors, he decided to go and get acquainted with Onkel Hans.

One day, Harvey said to me, "I'd like to take you home to Texas with me."

I thought I knew what he meant, but I acted clueless.

"How could that be?" I asked, wide-eyed.

"Well," Harvey said, "we could get married."

"I don't know," I replied. "I will have to ask my mother."

"What if I drive up to Dachau and ask Onkel Hans?" Harvey asked.

That sounded fine to me, but Onkel Hans told Harvey that my mother must be consulted. My stepfather wrote to my mother through the Red Cross and told her he liked Harvey and he spoke German.

We started working on a plan to reunite my family. Mutti wanted to join the three of us so much that she arranged to cross from East Germany to West Germany in the south. Coming to West Germany illegally was still very difficult and dangerous in early 1946.

Harvey got word that she would attempt to cross the border near the small village of Kronach, where he should meet her about the 10th or 11th of February. Mutti's trip went according to plan.

Harvey brought Mutti to Maisacher Strasse where I lived and she stayed with the neighbors because the Schmidt house was so small. Then Harvey went to Dachau and arranged for my stepfather to get passes for three or four consecutive days. Harvey picked him up each morning and took him back to the prison each afternoon.

During that time, Harvey formally asked my mother for permission to marry me.

Mutti said, "Well..."

Even though she liked Harvey, she was hesitant. She talked back and forth with my stepfather, who didn't have too much to say. He thought Harvey was a good person, which was the most important thing.

"Texas is so far from Germany," she told Harvey and me.

Then she agreed, adding, "You may never return, Renate. I may never see you again."

We celebrated my mother's birthday on the 13th of February, Harvey's birthday the 16th of February and our engagement all at the same time. Since food was still rationed, we had no cake or even a comfortable, quiet place to sit and visit. Nevertheless, we were together. It had been a long time since I had been that happy. I was sorry to see her return to Bad Berka.

When other people heard that I was going to marry an American, they said to me, "Why? Aren't there enough guys here?"

The comments hurt, but I loved Harvey and he was a respectable man.

Harvey expected to be sent home to Texas after he was released from his military service on the 20th of June 1946. After several years in Europe, he was ready to head back to Texas. He had already written and told his parents that he had met a German girl whom he wanted to marry. He said his family was happy for him and looked forward to meeting me.

In February 1946, Harvey and I went to see the Lutheran church pastor to seek permission to get married at Easter weekend, Saturday the 20th of April. I had a seamstress make me a plain blue and white dress. We were so excited.

Then we were told that the wedding was impossible. We would not be permitted to marry because Harvey was an American soldier and I was a German civilian.

"No problem," Harvey said. "We'll get married after I am discharged. Should we set a date?"

Sunday the 28th of July sounded fine to me. I hoped my mother and my stepfather could come, but it would be too risky for Mutti to attempt to cross the East German border again so soon. My stepfather didn't know when he would be released from Dachau so that was that.

Before Harvey got his discharge, he applied for a civilian position with the American military. He was hired by the civil censorship division and from then on, he could eat at the officers' club on an American base and wear civilian clothes. He often wore his uniform, though, because civilian clothes were hard to come by. ♪

CHAPTER X
....

Immigration Plans Implode

S ome of us wondered if Harvey might stay in Germany after he became a civilian. I hoped he would, but Harvey's mother wrote asking when he would be home all the time.

Assuming we would have plenty of time before our wedding date of the 28th of July, we applied to the Germans and the Americans for permission. We had no problem getting permission from the Lutheran Church.

It was when we were waiting for the American permit that the bottom fell out of our plans once more. Our request was denied because the authorities said I had a party number.

"Did you know that?" Harvey asked.

Of course not, I had no idea. The idea sickened me and infuriated me. I hated the Nazis as much as my parents and the vast majority of German civilians.

"Harvey, it can't be. I had nothing to do with the party! I was a student nurse."

I was heartsick. There must have been a mistake. This seemed impossible. When I inquired, I was told that every girl my age who enrolled in the Hitler Youth was assigned a number when she turned 18. What would my mother and stepfather think?

Harvey believed me, thank God. Had he been less committed to our relationship, this news would have given him a reason to walk away. Because he trusted what I told him, I loved him even more.

"Let me check on it," he said. He went to his friend, who was an American officer, but even with a letter of recommendation from Lieutenant Lang, Harvey got nowhere.

But he wasn't giving up. Wearing his American army uniform, Harvey traveled to the former party headquarters in Berlin. There he was allowed to enter the bunker where the identification cards were stored in alphabetical order.

"I held your identification card in my hand. You wouldn't believe how I felt," he told me.

He felt a strong urge to either tear it up or slide it in his pocket, but he knew that was wrong. He put my card back in its place and walked out. Rules were rules and the rule was that an American citizen could not marry a German with a party number.

I would have to be denazified.

Harvey was told the denazification process could take up to two years. Until the investigation into whether I was guilty of any wrongdoing was completed, I couldn't get an exit permit. That meant I couldn't leave Germany legally because our marriage was not recognized by the American government.

In the meantime, we were married in the Lutheran Church on the 28th of July 1946. I went to live in temporary housing, a little wooden garden house with an outdoor toilet on the river close to Munich. There was one bedroom with two beds. I had a mattress, but no pillows and no blankets. I slept under one cover, a big bath towel. The little house had a stove, a nice little kitchen with pots and plates.

On weekends, Harvey would drive out from Munich where he worked and bring food. Helga, the girl who lived with Mutti in Bad Berka, crossed the border from East Germany and came to stay with me, the one safe place she knew of in West Germany. I still had ration cards and could pick up milk every day in my milk can; I think it was less than a quart each trip.

In August 1946, Harvey was transferred to Kulmbach, which was close to the Russian border, and put in charge of the motor pool. He also had access to an apartment where he, Helga and I lived. The front of the building faced the main street, while the back faced the motor pool and a courtyard. On the balcony, we kept our milk and butter cool since we had no refrigeration. The apartment had two bedrooms, a living room, kitchen and a nice bathroom. The living room was sparsely furnished, although we had central heat and a stove.

We got a couple of beds and Harvey got mattresses. How, I'm not sure; he may have traded cigarettes for them. We added a little bit at a time until we made the place comfortable. I still needed so much – pillows, sheets, blankets, towels.

About three months before our daughter, Evelyn, was born, my mother again made the treacherous crossing from the Eastern Zone to see us in the Western Zone. She brought me some pillows, which were light and easy to carry. Mutti found our living conditions very, very primitive because I had so few belongings.

When she crossed the border back into East Germany, she made a point of seeing Peppi. "Please go to Renate and help her. She needs you."

Before long, we got a short letter from Peppi telling us to pick her and her daughter up in Bebra on a certain date, although no arrival time was stated. This was the first letter I'd had from Peppi since the end of the war. The last time I had seen her, I picked up the silverware and painting to be given to my half-brother, Wilhelm. The thought of being with Peppi again excited me, but I was also concerned.

"How are you going to pick up Peppi?" I asked Harvey.

"No problem," he replied. "I'll get a jeep from the motor pool and drive to the train station. What does Peppi look like?"

I didn't have a picture so I tried to describe her.

"She is not fair and she's not dark," I said. "She has bluish grey eyes. She is about my height, a little heavier maybe, and she'll have a little girl with her."

"Don't worry, I'll find her," Harvey said.

Thank goodness, the Americans always had good communications so Harvey found out the daily train running from East Germany got into Bebra at 6 o'clock in the evening. When he couldn't get a jeep that day, he drove a big army truck to the train station and wore his army uniform. He told me later that the train station was dark, dingy and not very clean.

A woman rushed up to him and asked, "Are you Harvey?"

"Yes. Are you Peppi?"

Harvey must have been very relieved to find Peppi and Kristel.

Several hours later, they got to Kulmbach. I was so happy to see them all.

"Oh," Peppi said, laughing. "That Harvey drove like mad!"

Peppi looked around our quarters as if she was taking inventory and then went to work. Leaving Kristel with me, it seemed like she traveled all over Germany by train to get us things we needed. She had many connections through her husband, Erich, and made the most of them. Peppi had such a nice manner that it helped her get things done. People wanted to help her.

"Let me see your clothes," she said. Peppi wasn't satisfied with the few items I had left to wear.

"Harvey, could you please get me some more blankets?"

So Harvey got some more blankets and Peppi made me a gorgeous suit out of one of them.

After that, Peppi really got rolling. Harvey had to get this and Harvey had to get that. It worked! Peppi gave him orders, Harvey got Peppi what she wanted, and he didn't mind. Was there anything my

Peppi couldn't do?

Peppi had a lot of questions and concerns that she shared with Harvey. "What will your American family think when they find out the girl you have married was assigned a party number when she was a child? How will they treat her?"

Harvey foresaw no problems. "I'm a German and she's a German," he said. "I was born in the United States, but Renate can become an American citizen once she's over there."

These discussions were very painful for me, although I wanted to know where I stood. Harvey and Peppi always got along very well.

The happiest day of my life was when our daughter, Evelyn, was born in Kulmbach. I think it was also the happiest day of Harvey's life. We gave Evelyn the second name of Elisabeth, in honor of my beloved half-sister, Peppi. Evelyn was such a good baby.

Harvey registered Evelyn at the American consulate as his child. We led a normal family life except I could not go to the PX and commissary on the base to buy groceries and supplies. Harvey tried to shop for me, but it didn't work out too well. He brought home little cans of baby food that Evelyn wouldn't eat. Even when I sent him with a list, he couldn't seem to figure out sizes of clothing for her. Sometimes, he brought home such ridiculous things that I laughed because if I hadn't, I would have cried. For Christmas and Evelyn's first birthday, he got our little girl toy cars for little boys. We didn't have much money so it was so disappointing not to be able to get what I needed for Evelyn. There was still almost nothing to buy in Germany unless you traded on the black market.

We traded cigarettes or soap (or whatever else we had) to buy most of our food on the black market before and after Evelyn was born. I had plenty of fresh milk for Evelyn. Harvey traded cigarettes for my first diamond ring and I traded cigarettes for my first tablecloth. We got along fine and we were very happy together.

When my stepfather received word that he would be discharged from Dachau in the fall of 1947, we discussed whether he could be released to Kulmbach where we were living. Harvey and I told him repeatedly that the Russians would not allow him to resume operation of the health spa in Bad Berka. But it was no good; Onkel Hans wouldn't listen.

That proved to be the biggest mistake of his life.

When the Russians moved into East Germany, they viewed all businesses, even those that were small, to be needless, capitalist ventures.

My stepfather's health spa, like so many others, was confiscated. What had once been my father's nursery business was confiscated, too.

The Russians put my stepfather to work in a cement plant pushing cars of sand by hand. No longer a young man, the heavy manual labor took a toll on both his mental and physical health.

It wasn't just Onkel Hans who lost his business. His father, Herr Saenger, had been a very successful businessman before the war in Leipzig, where he owned a whole block of buildings. He had his own car and driver and wore such fine clothes that the inside of his winter coats were fur lined. Herr Saenger's second wife had a son who had been killed in World War I. She saved all of young officer's belongings including his gun, in a chest. When the Russians searched the premises, they found it, which was a very bad thing because all guns had been confiscated. All of Herr Saenger's businesses were seized and he was jailed.

When we heard stories like this, it is no wonder that Harvey didn't want me to take five-month-old Evelyn to meet Oma and other relatives. I realized that crossing the border from the Western Zone to the Eastern Zone was very, very risky, but I wanted to show our daughter off. Because Harvey was an American, there was no way he could go with me.

I also wanted to help my mother because things were not good in East Germany. In preparation for my trip, I removed the mattress from Evelyn's baby buggy and put in an extra mattress filled with 15 cartons of cigarettes. Then I placed the original mattress back on top. Evelyn rode a little bit high with all those cigarettes beneath her, but Mutti needed the cigarettes to trade for food and goods.

The day we left, Harvey watched us pass the American checkpoint, which was less than half a mile from the Russian border. He didn't budge from where he stood until he saw the Russian guards let me into East Germany. He must have wondered if he would ever see either Evelyn or me again.

I was so happy to be going home! I had to change trains, but a porter lifted the baby buggy into a rail car where they also stored bicycles. The old seats in the train were around the outside walls so we faced one another. Those trains were very slow, but I made it home to my mother in Bad Berka. It was a wonderful visit, but too soon, it was time for Evelyn and me to return to Harvey in West Germany.

Mutti was glad to get the cigarettes I had smuggled in for her. She traded them to get the house painted and a new fence built all the way around the property. She even sent me a picture to show what the cigarettes had bought.

The second time that I made a trip home to Bad Berka, Evelyn was just over a year old. I doubled the number of cigarettes that I smuggled into East Germany. Evelyn was sitting even higher in the baby buggy than on our first trip, but the Russian soldiers felt good about us because she was looking around, happy and smiling. They didn't give us a problem. On the way back, I traded the baby buggy for a beautiful stroller. Evelyn looked adorable in it.

Onkel Hans and my mother lived through those early bleak years in East Germany with the help of those cigarettes, which she shared with Oma. Oma wasn't as desperate for food because she had her own chickens, rabbits, a cow and a garden. ♪

CHAPTER XI

....

America at Last

By the spring of 1948, Harvey had a job in the PX in Nurnberg and we were living in American Civilian Occupied Housing there. I checked on my exit permit regularly, but it seemed that everything had become so difficult. What would happen if I never received an exit permit? We talked about it all the time and I stayed upset, so tired of all the rigmarole regarding the denazification process. I longed to go home, but I no longer knew where I belonged. I had a child and Evelyn was listed on Harvey's passport, not mine.

Running short of patience one day, Harvey told me, "If you don't want to come back to Texas with me, I will take my child and go home."

Then Harvey, Evelyn and I took a vacation in May 1948 with his boss, Lieutenant Lang and his German girlfriend, and we had a nice time. I returned to Nurnberg a little more relaxed. There was great excitement when we learned that while we were gone, the consulate had called Harvey. When he called back, he learned our prayers had been answered. The American army had decided to grant my exit permit that would enable me to leave Germany with Harvey and Evelyn.

One excerpt from the multi-page report read, "Investigations make clear that the defendant has been a member of the German Girl's Association for four years, but she did not acquire party membership. She has been recorded as a candidate only. It has been noted that the defendant did not hold either rank or position and did not show any objectionable or brutal conduct at any time."

Major William Chartock of the Nurnberg Military Base stated, "The proposed marriage will not bring discredit on the military service. Applicant and fiancé have been informed that this application relates only to military approval of the contemplated marriage and that they must make their own inquiries as to the requirements laid down by local civil law. Local investigation into the character and moral background of the German fiancé has been made and no derogatory information was disclosed. Interview of both solder and fiancé by the chaplain has been done and a recommendation of the chaplain is attached."

The base chaplain, Captain Charles R. Loss, wrote, "I have interviewed EES-Civ. Harvey W. Meiners, Nurnberg Military Post, and his fiancé, Renate Macherauch, German civilian, and find that they have known each other since September 1945 and have been formally engaged since April 1946. Both applicants are of the Protestant faith. Mr. Meiners will depart for ZI in August 1948. In my opinion, this marriage will not bring discredit to the military service nor be contrary to public interest. I recommend approval of this marriage."

With these documents in hand, Harvey and I were married, for the second time, on the 28th of July 1948. We left the port of Bremerhaven on the 28th of August onboard a commercial steamship, the SS Bienville, headed for Wilmington, North Carolina.

I was happy, yet my mother's words played over and over in my mind.

"You'll never return. We'll never see you again."

I watched the German shoreline gradually disappear, knowing that it was quite possible that it might be the last time I would ever see it.

Our cabin, which was on the outside of the boat, had four bunks. I slept on the lower bunk across from Evelyn and Harvey slept on the bunk above Evelyn. When the ship hit rough sea, Evelyn would get out of bed in the morning and the sway would take her all the way to my bunk. How she would laugh! The water line was only a couple of feet below the railing, which Evelyn was just old enough to climb. She loved the water so we had to watch her constantly.

When we went to eat in the mess hall, we passed by the officers' cabin. Evelyn, who charmed the crew and passengers, was intrigued with a typewriter that belonged to one of the officers. He would take her on his lap and, much to her delight, let her type.

Other passengers onboard were a husband and wife and their tiny baby, and another lady traveling alone. It was a good crossing that took two weeks.

On the 16th of September 1948, we arrived in Wilmington where we were met by immigration officials. Harvey and I had met on the 14th of September 1945. So much had happened in our lives in three short years.

The men stayed with the children at the train station while we three women - one Swiss and two German women - who were not citizens were taken to the police station to be fingerprinted and registered. We were treated so well. My first impression of America was very positive. When we returned to the train station, there was Evelyn sitting on the steps and patting her hands together in the dirt. She was having a fine time!

Evelyn only had two dresses, three pairs of socks and one pair of high top shoes. Although she had another pair, one had been lost en route. She was getting smelly by then because I couldn't easily do laundry and the trip had upset her potty training routine.

Before we left Wilmington, I said, "Harvey, we have to buy Evelyn some more socks. Is there a clothing store nearby?"

So we bought Evelyn some socks that cost 29¢ a pair. Harvey was horrified at the price. "That's too much money," he said.

We boarded the Southern Pacific Railroad for an overnight trip from Wilmington to New Orleans. Evelyn and I slept in the upper bunk and Harvey in the lower.

Looking out the window, everything was so new to me. I couldn't believe what I was seeing – wide open prairies and no houses, no people, nothing.

When we arrived in Houston at the train station on Washington Avenue, Harvey's sister, Vadie and her husband, Archie Oeser, as well as their nine-month-old son, Gary Dean, were there to meet us. Vadie and Archie loaded us up in their new vehicle, a very small black 1948 pickup truck. My sister-in-law spoke to me in German and I felt good about that. I didn't realize it at the time, but I would turn to Vadie repeatedly in the coming years for help and advice.

"Could we stop at a store?" I asked Vadie. "Evelyn needs something clean to wear,"

We pulled up in front of Weingarten's on Washington Avenue. When Vadie and I walked in, I stopped in shock. I was speechless. What I saw in Weingarten's was unbelieveable. Much of my teen and young adult years in Germany had been during and after the war when goods such as clothing were not available and food was always scarce. Bright lights shone everywhere. I remember that sight even today, 64 years later.

Enjoying the look on my face, Vadie said, "The groceries are upstairs and the dry goods downstairs."

Glancing through the racks I soon found what I needed – a new dress for Evelyn that cost $3. I also bought another pair of socks for 29¢. I was hoping we would be able to wash clothes right away. Again, when I told Harvey how much the clothing cost, he grumbled that it was terrible to have to pay so much for one pair of little girls' socks.

When I wrote back home to my family in Germany soon after we arrived, I told them all about our trip. I said when we stopped at a store in Houston they could not imagine the luxuries available. It was beyond my wildest dreams.

Everything a person could want was in that one store. I was not accustomed to seeing that in Germany where there were many individual small merchants.

Vadie and Archie took us home that night to their little home on Lang Road, which is now called Bingle Road, in west Houston. It was way out of town in those days. Their house had one very small bedroom, a small living room and equally small kitchen, but it was comfortable and clean. We huddled together visiting. Then Archie got out a big, round pot that he called a washtub and set it in the middle of the living room. He heated water on the stove so I could bathe Evelyn. She was 18 months old and wasn't accustomed to this situation. She didn't want me to undress her; she didn't want me to put her in the tub either.

The others finally said, "We better go and leave those two alone." They went outside until after I had finished bathing Evelyn. Then the guys took the tub and poured the water out the door. I found it all very interesting. It was all so new to me. The primitive part didn't bother me. I felt like I could handle it.

Besides Vadie, Archie and Gary Dean, a Houston newspaper reporter had been there to meet our train. The next day his article read, *"On his first day in Germany with the army of occupation, Harvey W. Meiners was looking over the town of Eschwege when he spotted a tall brunette girl standing in the doorway of a home.*

"What are you waiting for?" he asked in German.

"For you," she said in German."

Most of the story was correct, although he dramatized how Harvey and I met a little too much. Toward the end of the article, the reporter quoted me as saying I was fascinated by the bright lights of the American cities, the department stores and the food. He added that someday, I hoped to bring my parents here. He was right about that.

After spending the night with Vadie and Archie, the next morning we got in the pickup and started the 100-mile drive out to Fayette County to meet Harvey's family. Vadie drove and Evelyn sat between us, while I held Gary Dean on my lap. There were no car seats for children in those days. Harvey and Archie sat in the back of the truck all the way. I don't know how fast Vadie drove on Hempstead Road and through towns like Brenham, but probably the speed limit. The trip seemed to take forever.

During the drive, I compared everything I saw to what I had known in Germany. I decided the countryside looked nice. I thought the houses looked a little primitive because I wasn't used to seeing them built on blocks. The streets were okay, but not as good as those in Germany.

After we left the main highway, the roads wound around and around in the countryside that seemed largely deserted. I had never seen such a big prairie like this. In Germany, every two or three miles there was a little village with a church steeple surrounded by clean, nicely cultivated fields. Here were miles and miles of wide-open spaces.

Had I arrived at the end of the world? I was a little bit scared and then a flood of homesickness washed across my heart.

Harvey's parents greeted us so nicely, though. His mother was overjoyed to see her boy after four long years. Harvey's grandparents, Lina and Willie Schellberg, were there to greet us, too. They spoke German with just a few English words thrown into their vocabulary. We were all standing outside when all of a sudden Grandpa Meiners appeared from inside the house. He looked like a gentleman in work clothes. Delvin, Harvey's younger brother was there, too. The whole family welcomed me so warmly; they wanted me to feel at home.

When they first lifted Evelyn out of the truck, she was gone chasing after the chickens. Peep, peep, peep. She loved those birds and wasn't afraid of them. Years later, her great-grandparents teased her that she wouldn't even take a good look at them when she arrived in Fayette County. All she wanted to do was follow the chickens around the yard.

When Harvey introduced Evelyn to his parents' dog, she got down on her knees and played with it. She was as happy as she could be. I couldn't believe my eyes; my little girl was playing in the dirt.

I don't mean to be critical, but the Meiners' house was so different from what I had been used to in Germany. There was no indoor plumbing and water for use in the house was collected in a cistern. Water for the cattle was pumped from a well. It didn't taste good because there was subsurface lignite in the area. The Meiners had no electricity and a party-line telephone that had to be hand cranked. The lane leading to their house was partly graveled and partly dirt.

But, oh my, Harvey's mother was a good cook. I couldn't remember the last time I had eaten such fine food. Mama Meiners had a big garden with every vegetable we could think of in it. Since Evelyn was little, she didn't eat everything that was put on the table, but we got along fine. She had plenty of milk to drink and fresh butter to eat, too. I had churned butter at Oma's house in Germany so I was glad to have a chance to do that again.

A local custom that amazed me was that on Friday night, Harvey's mother would hand him a blue enamel bucket. He would take it to Nechanitz and come back with that bucket half-full - and sometimes more than half-full – of fresh meat. The Meiners were members of a beef club. Everything was so new to me.

A day or two after our arrival, Harvey's mother scolded me.

"You can't wash every day," she explained. "We have to be careful with water or we won't have any."

"I can't let my child go dirty," I countered. Evelyn didn't have many clothes, but she didn't really need more because I had been washing them every day. I wanted to please Mama Meiners so from then on I didn't wash as often, which made me a little anxious.

We took our baths in a round tub. Three of us used the same water. The baby went first, then the mother, then came the father. I didn't mind this too much because I realized the family saved water this way.

The Nechanitz Store was not very far, so I took a walk there every day. It was very primitive compared to what I had once been used to, but it had everything that I could imagine and the owners, the Matejowsky family, was very nice to me.

The Lutheran church at Waldeck was also very different to me, too, because the men sat on one side and the women on the other. They didn't do that in Germany.

Never had I seen roads like those in Fayette County. The road from the Lutheran church at Waldeck to the Nechanitz Store had wagon ruts as deep as 18 inches. The roads were mud or dust depending on the weather.

The first week we were in Fayette County, we spent a whole day traveling the 12 miles to La Grange and back on those narrow, dusty gravel roads. We went to Prause's Meat Market and stood up eating crackers and meat. They were so sweet to me. How different that was from Germany! People in La Grange were aware that I came from Germany and before I could practice my limited English, they would speak to me in German. That, of course, made me feel good.

Soon after we arrived, we visited first one relative and then the next, and then visited one neighbor and then the next. Everybody spoke German and treated me royally, but their names and how they were related or where they lived had begun to run together in my mind.

"Aren't you glad you're in Texas?" they all asked me. They were aware of how tough conditions were in Germany after the war.

"Yes, yes," I would reply, but I really wasn't. I wanted to go back home to Germany. I was homesick. Oh, I was homesick, so homesick. At the very least, I longed to be alone with my husband and child.

One afternoon, Mama Meiners told me, "We are going to have company this evening."

"That sounds nice," I replied. "Who is coming?"

"There's going to be a shower for you and Harvey."

What was Mama Meiners talking about? I had no idea. I was absolutely clueless. I thought a shower was when you bathed standing up. I went to find Harvey and ask him what this meant.

He laughed and explained, "When a couple gets married, the neighbors come and bring gifts. They call them shower presents."

This was new to me. I went back to ask my mother-in-law more questions about why this shower was taking place.

"They want to welcome you," she said.

"How many people are coming?" I inquired. The Meiners house had only two bedrooms, along with a dining area and kitchen together. Mama Meiners never answered my question. She was too busy untying her apron.

"Oh, they are coming now," she said. "Let's go and meet them."

Clouds of dust boiled up from the dirt road as one car after another drove into the yard until there was nowhere left to park.

"How will they all get in the house?" I wondered to myself. "There isn't room. It's impossible."

When Harvey introduced us, each person welcomed me in German and we shook hands. It was a nice feeling. I had already met Ora Nell and Joe Matejowsky and their family at the Nechanitz store. Others who came with their families were Ella and Ernst Weishuhn, Elsie and Wildon Weishuhn, Willie and Adele Speckels, Earl and Alice Stork, Edna and Alvin Mueller, Leonie and Elton Wolff, Willie and Johanna Busch and Elton and Milda Albers, along with Enno Wehrmeister. Some were dressed nicely in their Sunday clothes, while others wore clean work clothes. Their arms were filled with plates of food and presents. Some were tied simply with pretty ribbons.

Over and over, their first question was, "How do you like it here?"

"Okay," I replied.

"Aren't you glad to leave Germany?"

I swallowed hard. I could hardly speak. They meant well, these kind, generous people. If they had only known how homesick I was, though, perhaps they would have been disappointed in me.

The men disappeared outside and the women came indoors. Every chair was full. The beds were pulled a little back from the walls so the ladies could sit all the way around them. Each room was filled with women and children. I had never seen a big group in someone's home before.

Talk, talk, talk, talk. They wanted to know exactly where I was from and about our trip from Germany. Then they told me where their ancestors came from, which was interesting to me. Most of these people were second or third generation Americans. Only a few had come from Germany as small children.

When it was time for Evelyn to be put to bed, there were so many people in the house that there was nowhere to put her down for the night.

The guests brought so much wonderful food with them: pies, cakes, sandwiches, my first taste of potato chips, salad, meats, but no alcohol.

They told me to unpack the goodies on the bed so they could see what gifts I had received. There were pillowcases, dishtowels, towels, doilies, pots and more. The shower was wonderful and, at the same time, a little overwhelming. I thanked the guests for their gifts and for coming that evening.

About a week later, we started to make the rounds to visit all the people who had come to the shower. They were still picking cotton around in Fayette County, but Sunday was a day of rest. One of the couples we visited was Tante Bertha and Onkel Gustav Wolff. Since they lived close-by, we went in the evening. Onkel Gustav didn't say much, letting Tante Bertha carry on the conversation.

Tante Bertha was different. She didn't say, "Aren't you glad you are here?"

At one point during the visit, she pointed at me and indicated that I should follow her. She was the only one who had beckoned me like that. The others had said something like, "Would you like to see my house?"

I followed Tante Bertha into the next room where a big wooden cabinet stood against the wall.

She said, "I want to show you something." When she opened the heavy oak doors, the upper shelves were filled with material, the most beautiful selection of fabric I had ever seen.

"Those are feed sacks," she told me.

"Wow!" I was impressed. Again, the shortages in Germany flashed through my mind.

I had no idea what a feed sack was, however, so Tante Bertha explained that feed for the chickens and flour for the kitchen all came in feed sacks. I was under the impression she was a seamstress who sewed for other people, but the feed sacks were hers and hers alone.

I liked that cotton material because it looked a little like linen, which was familiar to me. I realized that I had received hand-embroidered pillowcases made from feed sacks at my shower. The pillowcases were not the right size for German pillows, though, which were much bigger in size. I had so much to learn and understand.

Harvey's cousin and her husband, Gladys and Ernst Schwartz, who lived in Houston, invited us to come and celebrate my 21st birthday with them. Gladys invited their closest relatives in Houston and had a huge decorated cake for me. I felt so special.

After we'd been in Texas two weeks, we were notified that the new Ford car we had bought in Germany had been delivered to New York. We decided when we went to get it that Evelyn would stay with Harvey's parents. She would be in good hands. At that time, all she was interested in was the chickens anyway.

Harvey's grandmother was nicknamed Muna and his grandfather called Fader. Muna loved to touch Evelyn and tell her repeatedly, "You were born in Germany."

When she heard about our plans to leave Evelyn with her grandparents, Muna asked, "Can I keep Evelyn, too?"

"No," Mama Meiners told her, "you don't have a baby bed. Your beds are too high and Evelyn might fall off and hurt herself."

"We will make a bed," Muna said.

Harvey thought Evelyn would be fine with his grandparents. "Let Muna have Evelyn for one night," he urged his mother.

So Harvey's grandparents were allowed to keep Evelyn one day and one night only. To ensure she was safe, they pushed the bed where Evelyn was to sleep against the wall and set two kitchen chairs right in front of it. There they sat all night watching that no harm came to her.

Harvey's parents drove us to the train station in Austin on the 3rd of October. We took along a lunch my mother-in-law made us in our little carry-on bag. It was steaks and gravy on homemade bread. Something like that really needs to be eaten on a plate with a spoon because it got soggy, but it tasted so good.

In early October, it was still very hot in Texas so I wore a light dress with a little bolero that had three-quarter length sleeves. When we changed trains in St. Louis, it was bone chilling cold. We slept overnight sitting up on those railcar seats. Sometime during the night, my feet started to get nice and warm so there must have been a heater. We picked up our car and got out of New York as fast as we could. It took us two or three days to get back to Fayette County.

When we drove into the Meiners' yard to show off our car, my mother-in-law couldn't wait to show me what she had done. Mama Meiners had made Evelyn four new dresses out of feed sacks.

"Thank you so much," I said, "But this is a waste of your time because Evelyn is going to outgrow them."

"No, no, no," Mama Meiners said. "When she does, I'll make her some more."

I wanted to go to La Grange by myself and see the stores because it was all so new and interesting to me.

"We will take you," Harvey said.

"No, I want to go by myself. Please Harvey, take me to La Grange and let me walk around by myself."

So we drove to La Grange. On the way, I rehearsed in English how to tell a sales clerk that I wanted to purchase two pairs of socks and two pairs of panties for Evelyn.

Harvey parked on the Square in front of the courthouse and gave me a little spending money. I walked into Gindlers Department Store and made my way to the children's department where the socks and panties were on display. A saleslady walked up behind me and asked in perfect German, "Can I help you?"

That surprised me so much that I forgot my limited English vocabulary and we started to converse in German. It seemed like everyone in La Grange knew who I was. I had no idea who they were, however.

I developed a terribly painful rash so Harvey took me to see Dr. Guenther in La Grange. Dr. Guenther spoke German. In fact, everybody seemed to speak German. He gave me some cream to put on the rash, but it didn't help. I later realized that I was probably suffering from a heat rash. I found the heat oppressive and was not dressed properly for it either.

"In Texas," Harvey told me, "You have to drink lots of water."

"No!" I said. "Oma told me never to drink water because I would get stomach lice."

Nothing Harvey could say would change my mind. Instead of water, I started drinking Kool-Aid and got very sick because it was so sugary. This was Oma's fault! She and Mutti always drank hot tea. The water was boiled for that. I had drunk hot tea in Germany, too. Germany imported coffee so we rarely saw it after the war started. Mutti would trade something to get 10 or 15 beans that would make about two cups of coffee. It had been such a treat back then.

But in Texas, I soon learned I had to drink water whether I liked it or not.

The first funeral that I attended in America was for Tante Toni Foltermann. When we got back from New York with our car, we received word that she had died from a stroke. I had met Tante Toni and Onkel Fritz, who lived right next to Gladys and Ernst, at my birthday party.

Harvey's mother said to Harvey and me, "Let's go and clean up the cemetery."

Clean the cemetery? That was something new to me because in Germany we would not have to do that. Cemeteries there were maintained like parks. By German standards, the Waldeck Cemetery, which had been established in 1866, was very new.

When we got there, I noticed it was surrounded by a plain barbed wire fence, I could see only the tops of a few tombstones because the grass and weeds were so high. It appeared that it had been a long time since anyone had been there. I was shocked, but could tell Harvey was at ease with the situation so I tried to cover my surprise.

"Where will Tante Toni be buried?" Harvey asked Mama Meiners.

"Over there," his mother said, pointing toward the back of the cemetery. Making a path as we went, we wound our way through the tall weeds in that direction.

"It must be here," Harvey's mother said, stopping beside the graves Harvey's great-grandparents, the Foldermanns.

So we went to work. I helped them pull weeds and rake them up in piles. Harvey used a scythe, not a lawnmower. We gathered up all the debris, put it into a big washtub, and emptied it outside the fence.

Then we drove to see a man from Round Top about coming out to dig the grave. We had marked the site for him.

"Please Harvey, I don't want to be buried here," I said. For me, it was too lonesome and wild a place to spend eternity.

Harvey explained to his parents very carefully afterward that the cemeteries in Germany were maintained like public parks. They seemed to understand. In fact, Mama Meiners was all for improving the looks of the cemetery.

"Will you help us?" she asked.

Yes, of course, we would help. We agreed to come ready to roll up our sleeves and get busy one day the following spring.

<hr />

While he was in the army, Harvey had sent home money to his father who had put it away for him. A house and a farm came up for sale in the Nechanitz community while we were staying with Harvey's parents. We had enough money for a down payment.

I couldn't tell Harvey "No," because this was his home, but I think he knew how I felt. He could tell I didn't like living in Fayette County. It wasn't Harvey's fault because he had not painted any glamorous pictures of rural life in America. He had been honest about what I should expect, but I had not envisioned everything would be so different from what I had known.

Imagine my relief when Harvey told his parents, "I'm going to look for a job in Houston."

Nothing took my homesickness away. I didn't complain to Harvey because I was treated so well. Nevertheless, for a long time, I prayed that Peppi would come and get me. She had been solving my problems since I was a child. But then again, Evelyn was so happy in America that I couldn't take her away, nor could I go away without her.

After I had been in Texas a few weeks, the United States Department of Justice Immigration and Naturalization Service sent me a letter in care of my father-in-law at Ledbetter, Texas.

It read, "As the Commissioner of Immigration and Naturalization of the United States of America, I cordially welcome you upon your arrival. Persons who come to make their homes in this country usually wish to become citizens when they have been here long enough. An applicant for citizenship (among other requirements) must be able to speak English, to sign the petition for naturalization, and to show understanding of the principles of the Constitution and Government of the United States.

The public schools in many cities and towns have classes for applicants to learn about these subjects. They will be very glad to help you. This instruction will make it easier when appearing before the naturalization examiner. I extend best wishes for your success in your new country. (Signed) Watson B. Miller, Commissioner"

I wanted to become a citizen as soon as I could do so. ☽

CHAPTER XII

Culture Shock

While I struggled with homesickness as a stranger in this strange land called Texas, the situation for my mother and stepfather behind the Iron Curtain in Bad Berka was very bleak. They had virtually no income and barely enough money for food.

Those were some of the worst days of my life. I felt so helpless.

Mutti wrote that Onkel Hans's father died about six months after he suffered a stroke in prison. After his father's death, Onkel Hans was lost. He said he couldn't live in the Eastern Zone any longer and fled to the Western Zone with a little bit of cash and a backpack of belongings. When Mutti was questioned, she said he had just disappeared. No one was supposed to know that he had left the Eastern Zone. Otherwise, they would have locked up my mother. Onkel Hans couldn't register for food stamps in the Western Zone because the authorities would have put him in a refugee camp. It wasn't long before he run out of money.

We were still staying with Harvey's parents in Fayette County and didn't have much money ourselves. However, when there's a will, there's a way. I went to the Nechanitz store and bought several pounds of Eight O'clock coffee and a carton of cigarettes to mail to Mutti.

I never discussed my mother's circumstances with the Matejowskys, but they must have heard about their situation through Harvey or my mother-in-law. The Matejowskys were so helpful and couldn't do enough for me. Charlie Matejowsky sold the coffee and cigarettes to me at just above his cost and saved extra packing paper and little boxes so I could wrap the coffee and cigarettes securely for him to mail. Including postage, the total cost was about $4.

The Russians let the packages through, although all mail took a long time to be delivered. From the sale of the coffee and cigarettes, Mutti saved some money and sent it to Onkel Hans, although not directly, but through his landlady. She couldn't address a letter to him in Bremen because she didn't want to divulge his whereabouts.

Since Harvey did not intend to work on the farm or buy a farm of his own, we made several trips to Houston to look for a little piece of land where we could build a house. We ended up buying two lots, about a 50x100-foot strip of land, from my sister-in-law and her husband. Harvey's uncle, Edwin Schellberg from Needville, Texas, helped him build our little square frame house that sat on blocks. It was the fifth house on the right side of Lang Road, about two miles from the Hempstead Road.

We arrived in Texas in September and by November, the roof was on our little house and the windows and doors had been installed so we moved in. It was not finished inside, however.

I asked Harvey, "Can we have a parquet floor?"

I'm not certain why I was so anxious to have a parquet floor. I must have seen it advertised and taken a great liking to it.

"Oh, sure," he said, but it was to be many years before I got my parquet floor and it was in a different house.

The floor in our first house had plain pine boards with lots of knots. I scrubbed that floor, I waxed that floor; then I scrubbed that floor and I waxed that floor some more. The walls were covered with a horrible product like cardboard called calotte.

We had electricity, though, and bought a stove and butane tank in Carmine so I could cook. Several days later, Vadie took us to downtown Houston where we bought an electric refrigerator at Foley's department store.

The little water pump outside was easy to operate and I had my clothesline so I could wash as much and as often as I wanted to. In the big kitchen sink, I could wash dishes and after I scrubbed it, I could bathe Evelyn there. We didn't have indoor plumbing, but I didn't care because our little family was under our very own roof and we had a telephone, a party line that served five families in the neighborhood.

We bought our first big order of groceries at Weingarten's on Washington Avenue for $23. At Sears on Washington Avenue, we bought a big frying pan and a little frying pan, a pot to cook our potatoes in and a little roaster. These basic kitchen utensils cost $28. That's how we started out.

Harvey's parents had given him a calf as a gift when he turned 18. By the time he returned from Germany that calf was grown and had a calf of its own. When we moved to Houston, Harvey wouldn't leave without them. He put them in a pasture beside our house on some land that didn't have a clear title.

Harvey soon got a good job as a machinist at Earl McMillan's shop that paid about $1 an hour. Although he worked 45 hours a week, his paycheck didn't stretch too far. I never considered myself poor, though.

Harvey never felt we were poor either. Maybe we didn't have a lot of money, but we always had love. I know saying that is considered a cliché, but it was the truth.

Even though a tankful of gas cost $3, we managed to drive out to Fayette County once a month to see Harvey's parents. They were so happy when we came. They couldn't wait to see how Evelyn had grown and hear what we had been doing. Each time we visited, I made a point of walking over to Matejowsky's store to buy coffee and cigarettes to mail to Mutti.

When Harvey, Evelyn and I would get ready to return to Houston, my mother-in-law always made certain we had fresh eggs and vegetables to take back with us. Every once in a while, she would give us a chicken she had just butchered. From Mr. Rauch who lived next door to Harvey's parents, we bought sausage.

By this time, I was much happier. I was starting to feel better about Texas.

I decided I should go to work and earn some money even though I was not yet a citizen. I was hoping and praying we could bring Mutti and Onkel Hans to Texas someday. Harvey was in total agreement with my plan. We were willing to sponsor my parents, but we needed the money to pay for their trip. That's why we were saving up.

I answered an ad in the paper to work at an ice cream cone factory on Hempstead Road. I had never worked in a factory, but it was fun. After three days, I realized I would have to quit because I had no reliable transportation to get to and from work. Harvey needed the car to go to his job and I couldn't drive. The bus didn't go that direction and the timing didn't work with our neighbor's schedule, although he was willing to take me. Thank goodness that Vadie always was willing to look after Evelyn.

Next, I called on our new telephone to answer an ad for a daycare facility on Washington Avenue in the Heights. I told the lady who ran the school about my training as a nurse and experience in babysitting small children. I also explained I had a three-year-old daughter. She was pleased with my background and said I could bring Evelyn with me to school.

I was so excited because I knew the bus schedule would work out for me to get there and back. I arranged for Vadie to drive me to the school for an interview the following day. When I got there, the lady said, "I thought you had changed your mind when you didn't come yesterday. I'm sorry; I have hired someone else."

My English was so poor that I had misunderstood that the manager wanted me to come right away.

Harvey sent me to Sears to buy a gallon of paint called Horizon Blue. The salesman sent me home with the wrong color because he couldn't understand me. I vowed that I would work on my English and I did.

* * *

Another weekend that spring, we came out to help clean up the Waldeck cemetery. When we pulled up, I couldn't believe it. All the weeds and dead grass in the cemetery had been burned off and all the stones were clearly visible now.

"What happened?" I asked Harvey's mother. "Didn't I see little wooden crosses here and there last fall?"

"Oh, yes," she said. "We picked up those crosses and put them in the little storage building before we started the fire. That dry grass burned so well."

But not all the crosses had been picked up and when it came time to put the little crosses back that had been gathered up, no one remembered exactly where they belonged. I felt very badly because I thought they had gone to all this effort to impress me that their cemetery could look as good as those that I had known in Germany.

Not long after the picture and write-up of our arrival appeared in *The Houston Press*, we were contacted by a German couple, Herr and Frau Hoffmann, who owned a plant nursery on Hempstead Road. They welcomed us and introduced us to a local German club dedicated to the cultivation and promotion of German music called the Houston Liederkranz. Members of the group were either German or of German descent. Harvey joined in August 1949 and I became a member the following November. There I met five other German war brides. Although we never sat down and talked about our experiences during the war years in Germany, we shared a common bond. I wore my costume that represented the German state of Thueringen to German Society events where we would sing. Over time, I collected about five costumes, including a Bavarian dirndl.

After I attended classes on South Main where I learned how the government operated, as well as how the American legal system functioned, I applied for American citizenship in 1950. I was impressed with the concept that the United States had a "government by the people, for the people." Yes, this is my kind of my country, I decided.

"You had better listen to her because she could teach you something!"

the citizenship examiner told my two witnesses when I went for my test. I was pleased. I couldn't wait to vote because I never had the opportunity to do so in Germany; I wasn't old enough.

My mother said when she voted in Germany during Hitler's time, she had to walk down a very narrow aisle with boxes on either side where you placed your ballot. A poll watcher beside the box recorded how she voted. She didn't want to vote after that, but my stepfather encouraged her to do so. Otherwise, it might have drawn attention to them and they would have had nothing but problems. There was only one party to vote for so why vote? It wasn't a free election. It was a dictatorship.

Oma passed away in 1952. Even though she never met Harvey, I was so glad that I had taken Evelyn to see her twice.

My third attempt at getting a job in Houston worked out somewhat better. I was hired at the DePelchin Faith Home, which sheltered orphaned children, by a German woman doctor from Hamburg named Dr. Pfeifer. She helped me with my reports that had to be completed in English and offered me lots of encouragement. I have never forgotten her kindness and support.

I worked the afternoon shift from 3 o'clock until midnight. Sick children would come to me in the infirmary in their pajamas to show me a sore finger, complain of a tummy ache or have a little bit of a temperature and I would take care of them. They were all so sweet. One little girl even brought me her cat. Yes, it was a real, live cat. She thought it had a broken leg so I made a little splint for her.

When we got to know each other better, Dr. Pfeifer said to me, "Why don't you go back to nursing school? We will help you pay for it and I will tutor you in English."

I couldn't wait to get home and tell Harvey that Dr. Pfeifer had recommended that I enroll at the University of Houston to finish my education. He was in favor of the idea, but transportation again was the issue.

We lived two miles away from the closest bus stop, which was a long walk twice a day. Sometimes I was able to catch a ride with a neighbor. Then I had to ride the first bus for about an hour and change to another bus on Washington Avenue to reach the stop that was closest to the DePelchin Faith Home. The distance wasn't that far; it was just hard to get there from where we lived.

For Christmas in 1953, Harvey gave me a bicycle so I could ride to the bus stop. That was my first bicycle and I was very pleased. When I was a child, I had ridden other people's bicycles, but had never had one of my own. Even though having a bicycle was an improvement, in the wintertime I was heading straight north. Going against a north wind was rough, especially if it was raining.

The bus came only about four times a day and didn't run at all in the daytime. It took me five hours one way to get to the University of Houston. On the return trip, I attempted to stop off at the DePelchin Faith Home, but the bus schedules made that next to impossible. I was so discouraged.

"Learn to drive and take the car," Harvey said, but I was afraid.

I felt sad, but I had to let the dream of completing my education go.

He would take four-year-old Evelyn across the street to Vadie's home in the late afternoon before he left for work at night. She stayed with Vadie until I got home. When I would get ready to leave for work, Evelyn would cling to me and cry that she didn't want to go to Aunt Vadie's house. She wanted to stay home and help me cook. Man, it was so hard to leave her that I decided to give up my job. I stayed at the DePelchin Faith Home only three months. Harvey agreed that Evelyn's happiness was more important. He was willing to work two jobs.

When I handed in my resignation, Dr. Pfeifer encouraged Harvey and me to adopt a three-week-old orphan boy named Leon. Leon was a good baby, so easy to care for, but the adoption was not approved because we had only two bedrooms in our little house – Evelyn's and ours. Leon would have had a good home with us.

After I became a citizen, Harvey started getting active in politics. I would watch the political conventions on television at night while he was working. I wasn't fluent enough to share my thoughts with him in English so I reported on the speeches in German.

I was registered to vote for the first time in the November 1952 federal election. Both Harvey and I took this obligation very seriously. On Election Day, we discussed the sample ballot first and then we voted separately. My heart was set on voting for Eisenhower, who went on to win a decisive victory by taking over 55 percent of the popular vote and winning 39 of the 48 states. He was the first Republican president in 20 years and had Richard Nixon as his running mate.

When we came out of the polling place, I said to Harvey, "You don't have to tell me how you voted."

"I didn't cancel your vote," he said. "I voted for the Republicans, too."

Papa Meiners, who was the Democratic precinct chair in Nechanitz, expected Harvey to one day take over for him. That's the way it worked in families. The next time we came to the country, Harvey told Papa Meiners that he had voted Republican. He expected to get an earful, but he didn't.

"Oh, okay," Papa Meiners said. "But I am still the Democratic chair here in Nechanitz."

Everything was fine between the two of them.

* * *

My mother wrote to tell me about the girl my cousin, Helmut, had married. Her name was Heidi and her story haunted me because her life in East Germany was such a contrast to mine in America.

In 1944, 10-year-old Heidi lived with her seven-year-old brother and her mother on the east side of Neisse River in Schneidermuhl, Poland. Her three-year-old brother, who was deaf, lived in an institution in the same city. Heidi's father had been drafted into the German army earlier in the war.

When the government authorities ordered residents of the city to leave their homes, her mother had only 15 minutes to pack some of their belongings. They were instructed to board a big truck across the river on the other side of the city. By doing so, they became refugees.

Heidi's mother panicked when she realized she had forgotten her warm coat. She got off the truck and rushed back across the bridge to her home to retrieve it. Before she could return to the truck where her children waited, the bridge was demolished. She had no way to get across the river. She was heartbroken that her children had been taken away and afraid because she had nowhere to hide.

Heidi and her brother were glad their mother's niece and her family were on the truck with them. The niece was told to take care of the two children traveling alone. After the refugees were loaded into empty railcars, they sat on the bare floors hugging their bundles of clothes. Like the orphan trains in Texas, the refugees got off wherever someone would agree to give them work. But who wanted two little children?

When the train stopped at Weissenfels, Heidi and her brother were the only ones left in the boxcar. The little boy was taken to an orphanage and Heidi was sent to work for a family. She washed dishes, scrubbed the floors and did other housework chores, as well as helped with the animals, whatever a 10-year-old could do. Never staying long in one place, she went from family to family, but she managed to stay in touch with her little brother for a long time. Eventually, she lost track of him. Heidi had no idea what had happened to her mother or her two brothers.

In 1952 at the age of 16, Heidi met my cousin, Helmut Bolling, who was an 18-year-old apprentice electrician. She had two goals. First, she wanted to get married so she would have a home of her own and second, she wanted to reunite her family.

After Heidi and Helmut were married, they set up housekeeping in a crudely constructed barn that had incurred bomb damage. Although Heidi could not write, she could read so she set out to find her brother through the Red Cross. She was successful and he came to live with her and Helmut. Also through the Red Cross, she located her deaf brother. The patients at that special school were taken out of East Germany much earlier than Heidi and her brother. When Heidi finally located her mother, the two were like complete strangers when they came face-to-face. Her mother was a broken woman who would not sleep behind a closed door because of the abuse she had suffered at the hands of the Russians.

How I wished I could have shared some of the wonderful gifts I had received as shower presents with Heidi. She had nothing but sheer determination to forge a better life for herself and her family. I admired her determination.

I got a job at Star Engraving on Waugh Drive in Houston where my German-speaking boss began teaching me the bookbinding business. I learned to gold stamp the covers of books and special printed materials on a new machine imported from Germany. The engineers who came to set it up spoke some English, but not much.

A week or so later, the owners told me, "Slow down!"

Several of my German war bride friends worked part time at Star Engraving during rush periods, but I was a full time employee. Every Friday night, Harvey would bring Evelyn and lift her up to look in the window of the room where we worked. My friends teased me about Harvey's regular as clockwork appearance before we were paid.

"Harvey can't wait to get his hands on your check," they said.

"Yes," I told them, "That's right, but there's a good reason why."

After we cashed my check, we would send some of the money to my stepfather in Bremen. He was living on the $10 he received every two weeks.

By early 1952, Harvey and I had saved enough money to bring Mutti to America. Things had gotten a lot worse for her in East Germany when the Russians informed her that she would have to move into a single room. The rest of the house was turned over to a family of six. In other words, her home had been confiscated. She worried all the time about Onkel Hans living in West Germany, too.

And I worried about them both and whether they would be content in America. They would find it so different from Germany, just as I had. What if they decided they wanted to go back? I wrestled to put my fears aside.

When Mutti left Bad Berka, she gave the police the excuse that she was needed in Leipzig to take care of her ill mother-in-law. She couldn't pack much luggage because she didn't want to alert the police that she was on the run. Instead of going to Leipzig, Mutti traveled to East Berlin where she stayed with Helga, the young woman who had lived with her some years before in Bad Berka. Through a coded message, I told her that we had a pre-paid airline ticket in her name waiting at the Lufthansa counter at the airport in the American-occupied sector. She crossed over to West Berlin on the subway. Her flight from Berlin to Bremen marked the first time she had been in an airplane. I had written Onkel Hans another coded message and let him know when he should go to pick her up. They were reunited for a few weeks before she boarded a freighter headed for America.

By that time, our Ford car was getting old and less reliable so Harvey's younger brother, Delvin, drove us to Mobile, Ala., in his Chevrolet. I was a nervous wreck until Mutti arrived safely on the 10th of March 1952.

"And you thought you'd never see me again," I told her as we hugged and hugged. What a relief!

What a wonderful reunion that was! I had not seen my mother for four long years. When we got back to Texas, Harvey's parents were so kind to my mother. They were happy that she had been able to get out of East Germany and could live in Texas for the rest of her life.

Harvey, Evelyn and I were still living in the little four-room house in Houston. Evelyn's room had gotten smaller because we had taken part of it to make a little front porch. She was still sleeping in a baby bed and we got my mother a cot. She slept with Evelyn in her room. We also started building a washhouse so, for the first time, I could have an indoor washing machine.

Right away, Mutti got a job working in the Hoffmann's greenhouse and was very happy.

Since Mutti had steady employment, we could set to work to bring Onkel Hans to America. During the process, some letters we received from him looked as if they were scribbled. They were not in his typical elegant handwriting. He complained that he wasn't feeling good, but after a few weeks, he said he was improving. We were concerned that he might not pass the immigration physical exam.

Onkel Hans finally arrived in Houston on a freighter in 1953. He and my mother rented a little house on the Hoffmann's property and were very content with their little home. Although it was virtually the size of a shoebox, it had every convenience including a bathroom. Of course, they loved living so close to us. Now they could watch Evelyn grow up.

My stepfather found work in the office at Herzog's lumberyard, but it didn't work out because his bookkeeping training in Germany was not consistent with American standards. So I arranged for Onkel Hans to come to work in the storage area at Star Engraving for a man named Archie who spoke German. They got along just fine and Onkel Hans enjoyed his work.

When he applied for a Texas driver's license, Onkel Hans never even had to take a test because the state recognized his German permit. By February 1957, he and Mutti had saved enough money to put a down payment on a new Volkswagen. Harvey went with Onkel Hans on a Tuesday morning to buy the car, get a loan from Heights Bank and purchase insurance. That evening, he and Mutti drove over to see us in their new VW. They brought a six-pack of beer along so the four of us could celebrate his new vehicle.

I had a driver's license by that time, too. The following morning, I thought to myself, "I don't have to pick Onkel Hans up today. He has a brand new Volkswagen to drive to work."

When I passed by the house where they lived, I noticed the Volkswagen was still under the shed. I had not been at work very long before my mother called from the Hoffmann's telephone to tell me to come quick. My stepfather's nose was bleeding badly. When I got there, he was sitting at the table with his head in his hands. I asked him, "What is going on?"

"Nothing," he said, "nothing."

But I knew something was wrong. He had suffered a stroke from which he never fully recovered. He had several more little strokes as well. Although I made more money than Mutti, we decided that I should quit my job in June 1958 to take care of Onkel Hans after his insurance ran out. She couldn't drive a car. If he needed to go to the doctor, she couldn't take him so I nursed him. He passed away on the 18th of December 1958.

Even though I left Star Engraving on good terms, I never went back there to work. They were fine people and I missed them.

By June 1963, we had finally saved enough money for Evelyn and me to go back to Germany for a visit. She was 16 years old at the time. Harvey, who had been employed at Cameron Iron Works for many years by then, didn't go with us because we didn't have enough money for three tickets. The cost of one airfare on Lufthansa was $700, which was a lot of money in 1963.

When Evelyn and I first arrived in Germany, we didn't like the food. We didn't like the people either. They weren't friendly, but seemed abrupt and rude. When I went to buy some apples at a stand on the side of the road, I picked one up.

"No, no, no," the Frau scolded me. "You don't pick them up."

After a couple of days, we started to adjust and began to like Germany better. We stayed three months and, of course, went from one relative to the next to visit. I was among my own people who treated me like a queen and Evelyn like a princess. I rekindled my special relationship with my half-sister Peppi, whom I had missed so much all the years I'd been in Texas. I told her that years before I had prayed that she would come, get me, and take me home to Germany.

"Why didn't you write me?" she asked. "I would have done that."

But I was glad that I hadn't.

I sent Harvey a letter asking if he could send us another $100 because we wanted to take a trip down to the Riviera. He did so and we appreciated the opportunity to visit that lovely area.

Evelyn loved Germany's green meadows as much as I did. She would sigh and say to me, "If only I had my Popcorn here." Popcorn was her horse.

When we took a tour of Buchenwald, it became very clear to

me how it had been divided into two separate areas – a prison and a concentration camp.

I found it hard to settle down when we returned to Houston. One day when I went to do my grocery shopping at Randall's on Mangum Road, I was driving along thinking to myself, "If I could only go back home."

I was homesick for Germany again.

That's when I ran into the car in front of me. I was furious with myself. I had no excuse. It was my fault because I wasn't paying attention. I had been daydreaming of Germany and not watching what I was doing. This was the first accident that I had ever had and I was ashamed.

What *was* I thinking? My husband, my daughter and my mother - everything I had ever wanted was right here in Texas! We had our own house and I had the choice of staying home with Evelyn or going to work. We had good friends and Harvey's relatives had always treated me so well. This country had welcomed me as an immigrant and allowed me to become a citizen.

Right then and there at the scene of the fender bender, I made up my mind. Yes, Germany would always have a special place in my heart, but Texas would be my home.

Since that day, I have never looked back. If someone told me tomorrow that I must go back and live in Germany, I would tell them, "Wild horses couldn't drag me there." ◡

Don't Fence Me In

There's an empty chair across from me now at the kitchen table. Harvey passed away of cancer at Easter in 2004.

Every day I miss him, but our love lives on in my memories. Harvey had lots of energy and ideas. He was always ready to try something new and he was a born leader. He enjoyed people and liked finding ways to connect with them. He was big hearted. We had such a good life together because I was always ready to get involved in whatever Harvey wanted to do. I found it interesting. Harvey was of the temperament that didn't handle being hemmed into a routine too well. At first, I didn't understand this, but later realized that was just the way he was made. Like every couple, we had our ups and our downs and sometimes, things didn't work out quite as we had expected.

We were shopkeepers for a while when we opened Harvey's Superette on Bingle Road in 1972. We spent all our savings and borrowed about $20,000 from friends to furnish and stock that little grocery store. We were also a drop-off point for Spring Branch Dry Cleaners and had a little feed store, as well.

Harvey opened the store at 7 o'clock and we didn't close until midnight every single night. That's when I began cleaning the store. I would tumble into bed about 2 o'clock and go back to the store a little after 8 o'clock. As soon as I got there, Harvey would leave to go to Borden's to pick up milk and other dairy products. He got very restless if he had to stay in the store all day. By that time, the clothes that people had brought in to be cleaned would be piled up for me to sort and I'd be busy waiting on customers all day. That store occupied my time practically 24/7 and it was exhausting even though I loved our customers.

Our house was about 150 feet behind the store. We installed an alarm system in the store that would wake up the whole neighborhood if it went off. Harvey had just opened the store at 7 o'clock one morning when he was held up at gunpoint. The alarm scared the robber and he ran off with about $30 from the till. The police never got him, but he didn't return either.

After we operated Harvey's Superette about six months, we realized that business wasn't too great for us or for the other neighborhood grocery store. Two stores in the same area was one too many. The owner of the other grocery also had a store in the Heights where I went to visit him.

"We want to expand," I told him. "How about selling us your store please?"

Two days later, we had his answer. "Yes."

We bought the second store on credit, too, of course. We operated both stores, which was a crazy, crazy time. Gradually, we took all of our groceries over to the other little store and converted our location into a pub. Although several different people operated it, it never really worked out so we sold it. Then we decided to sell the whole operation.

Using sewing samples and patterns that I had made an A grade on when I was 15, I talked my way into being hired as a seamstress for an elegant ladies dress store, Esther Wolf. It had been established in 1961 by Mrs. Esther Wolf in a quiet Houston neighborhood, which is now the busy Galleria.

I had no idea of what I was getting into at Esther Wolf. Mr. and Mrs. Wolf were Jewish and many of the words they used were similar to German. We never discussed it, but I concluded that they might have thought I was Jewish, too. I got along well with them.

When Mr. Wolf was meeting with a client, he would call me in to tell me how he wanted the piece of clothing altered. Then I followed his directions. One of the ladies I fitted was Miss Ima Hogg, a prominent Houston socialite, who was very careful with her expensive clothes. Rather than buy lots of new clothes each season, she had her existing garments altered to fit the style of that particular year. She was a very nice lady and treated me very well like the rest of my customers.

At my sewing machine, I sat beside another employee who came from Georgia. She often remarked, "I don't know what those darn foreigners are talking about."

"Well, Miss Mitchell," I would say, "I am a foreigner, too."

"Yes, but you are different," she would tell me and I would laugh to myself.

A male buyer from Tanner Fashions decided that I should dress in his line of clothing and model them on the floor of the store. I was allowed to take the articles of clothing home and keep them. Mrs. Wolf asked me to accompany her to Germany on a buying trip because I could speak the language fluently.

I loved that job – the clients, the work, everything about it, but by that time, my mother was in a wheelchair and needed my care. Harvey welcomed my decision to leave Esther Wolf. He wasn't crazy about my job. Perhaps he thought I would drift away from him.

Onkel Max came to see us in Houston on a three-month work permit. Under Russian rule, his fields in Germany had become "the people's property" so he could no longer farm them. An industrious man, he soon found work with a house builder as a cabinetmaker, which was his trade. He wanted to immigrate, but he had to go back to East Germany because he didn't have a green card. We were unable to take on the responsibility of supporting him in old age because he had no insurance and would not be eligible for social security. When he left, he padded the shoulders of his suit with American $100 bills. We tried to help him, but we could not. The look in his eyes when he left made me so sad.

Harvey and I visited Germany a number of times. My family and friends in the Russian zone treated him well. They accepted Harvey so completely that he became one of theirs. He liked to tease me that he was more German than I was.

With the help of the Red Cross, Harvey and Peppi finally located my half-brother, Wilhelm Macherauch. He had married a Canadian girl named Daphne, whose parents had emigrated from England. After their three boys started school, he changed the family's name to McMartin because no one could pronounce Macherauch. He was very pleased to receive the silverware and the painting that Peppi had saved for him from their father's home. Harvey and I visited Wilhelm and Daphne near Victoria on Vancouver Island, British Columbia, and they came to Texas to see us. We had a wonderful time. Harvey and I urged him to go back to Germany with us for a visit. I told him all our relatives wanted to see him, but he would never go. I don't think Wilhelm ever suffered from homesickness for Germany.

Mutti returned to Germany several times and stayed about three months on each trip. When she returned the second time, she said, "That's my last trip. I like it better here."

Some years later when she inquired about being eligible for compensation because the Russians had confiscated her house, she was told that she had no right to it. She had left East Germany without a permit. So that was that.

My father-in-law, Papa Meiners, passed away in September 1987 and Mutti passed away in October of the same year. During the last months of their lives, we cared for them here at home. By that time, we had left Houston and returned to the Nechanitz community in Fayette County.

Harvey was super with our parents. No one could have done more, but he couldn't be cooped up with two invalids 24 hours a day, seven days a week.

For example, one day Harvey told me, "I have to go."

"Go where?" I asked.

"I have to make a map of the Waldeck Cemetery," he said.

"Do you have to do it now?" I couldn't figure out why this was so urgent.

"I have to go," he repeated and off he went.

Indeed, he did have to go. Harvey told me later, "I admire that you can do it. I just can't." I forgave him right then and there. We've used that cemetery map ever since.

After the deaths of my mother and father-in-law, Harvey and I joined the docent organization at Monument Hill State Park in La Grange. Together we hosted a weekly Sunday afternoon German radio program on KVLG/KBUK in La Grange that had been started years before by Alex Wied. We taught German in continuing education classes in La Grange. So many participants signed up that we divided the group into two classes. Harvey taught one and I taught the other. Harvey was very active in the Round Top VFW and I participated in the auxiliary.

I transcribed the original handwritten records of many of the churches and cemeteries around this area for the Fayette County Archives in La Grange. I also translated the minutes written in German of who is buried where. There are still two unidentified graves outside the cemetery fence at Waldeck. We also have a list of people whose graves are not marked.

Harvey was always interested in politics and very well informed. We were very active during Barry Goldwater's campaign when he was the Republican Party's nominee for president in 1964. We went to the district convention across the street from the railroad station in Houston. It started at 6 o'clock in the evening and ended at 8 o'clock the next morning. From then on, Harvey got deeper and deeper into Republican politics and I helped him. In those days, the voting machines were still using rolls of paper. Harvey would have to crawl into the machines and give us the total number of votes each candidate got. Then the machines were picked up the next day or so and the votes were recounted. We never missed a convention for many years.

On June 12, 1987, President Ronald Reagan gave a historic speech in West Berlin toward the end of the Cold War. He said, "General Secretary Gorbachev, if you seek peace, if you seek prosperity for the Soviet Union and Eastern Europe, if you seek liberalization, come here to this gate. Mr. Gorbachev, open this gate. Mr. Gorbachev, tear down this wall!"

When it happened, I was lying down on the couch and Harvey was sitting in his chair watching the 10 o'clock TV news. We looked at each other and laughed. We couldn't believe that the wall would come down. If Harvey were here, he would tell you that I had a look of complete and utter disbelief on my face.

"You can close your mouth now," Harvey said. "It's true!"

How I wished my mother could have lived to see that!

Harvey served as county chair for the Republican Party in later years. I am still chairperson of the Fayette County Resolution Board and am sworn to treat everyone equal and I do so. My interest in politics has always been strictly from the standpoint that I had a choice of candidates. When someone comes to me and asks me why we have to vote for Republicans or Democrats, I tell them they ought to be glad. If there were only one party, we would be living in a dictatorship. I lived under Hitler's rule in Germany and it didn't work.

I recall when Harvey and I went to an American club when he was still in the army in Germany. Harvey would join the other soldiers as they sang one song repeatedly that Roy Rogers made famous in 1944. It was called *Don't Fence Me In.*

At the time, I took the lyrics literally: a cowboy wanted to ride across the open prairie. But now, I interpret the words a little differently because I prize my freedom.

My Photo Album

Renate Meiners

Located in the central part of Germany in the federal state of Thueringen, Germany, my hometown of Bad Berka on the Ilm River was a pleasant place in which to grow up between World War I and World War II.

Because my father died of tuberculosis, Mutti took me to be tested at this sanatorium pictured below every year. How I dreaded that checkup.

I am the only child of Johann Ernst Macherauch and Anna Marie Schmidt. My mother, whom I called Mutti, was 27 years younger than my father. This is the only picture I have of the three of us together.

Oma's cousin, Helene Jung, who was a famous soprano, performed in Dresden and regularly went on international tours before World War II. We were thrilled to be related to such a talented diva.

When I was a child, my mother and I crossed the Hexenberg, a high, forested plateau above Bad Berka, to visit my great-grandmother, Friedericke Kuenzel, in the village of Schoppendorf. She and my Great-Tante Anna, who is pictured below with Mutti, lived in a house built in 1780.

When my father's friend, Dr. Dobers (above left), agreed to serve as my godfather, he wrote my father an elegant acceptance letter (right). My mother introduced Dr. Dobers to his future wife, her friend, Charlotte. Mutti met Charlotte when she worked at the House of Medem in Weimar. Dr. and Mrs. Dobers are pictured above.

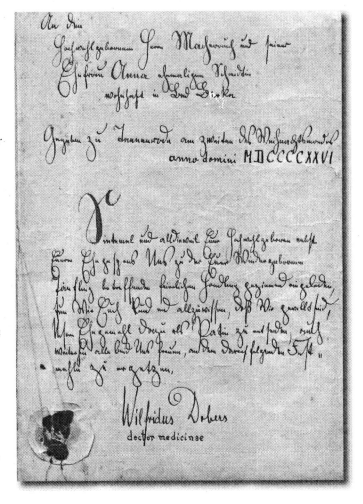

In my first grade class group picture (above), I am standing near the bunny toward the back of the class. The decorative cones were filled with wonderful Easter treats.

When I was 10 years old, a photo was taken of our entire class at school (below). I am the girl with the long braids sitting behind a boy with a checked shirt.

Memories Return After 50 Years

Renate Meiners, pictured in the inset, traveled to Eisenach, Germany recently where memories of 50 years ago returned after she found the statue for which she modeled when she was 12 years old. She is pictured on the left where she is seen with braided hair and holding an apple. The other models, the young man holding school books, and the teacher with his arms around the students, are unknown to Renate because the sculpturing was done separately. In 1938 she posed for the sculpture and found it again on her birthday, Oct. 2 in the city of many childhood memories. The inscription on the building gives the name of the school as it was known then. Today it is known as the public high school.

In 1938, my brother-in-law, well-known German sculptor Erich Windbichler, asked me to pose for a statue he was creating (left). I'm the little girl in pigtails on the left holding an apple. Sadly, Erich was drafted by the German army in 1940 and never returned. Today, the statue stands outside a school in Eisenach, Germany. These two photos appeared in The Fayette County Record on November 3, 1995. Photo courtesy of The Fayette County Record.

(Below) The picturesque Wilhelmsburg Hotel in Bad Berka was operated by a congenial Englishman named Herr Porter. When I was a child playing outdoors, he would often stop and ask if I'd like to accompany him. With Mutti's permission, I happily tagged along as he did his shopping in town. When Herr Porter brought me home, he always waited to see that I was safe in our yard before continuing his journey.

(At left) My older half-sister, Elisabeth, whom I always called Peppi, was my best friend for as long as she lived. I loved her dearly.

(Below) Those of us who joined Hitler's Organization of German Girls, the Jungmaedel, in order to participate in organized sports, wore a uniform to school that comprised of a brown skirt, white shirt and tie. I'm pictured on the second row at the far right.

In this picture taken in Mutti's garden at home, I'm in the center. My cousin, Inge, who lived with Oma Schmidt, is on my left and Camilla Dobers, the daughter of my godparents, is on my right.

My baptismal certificate shows I was confirmed on the 30th of March 1941, at the Marienkirche Church in Bad Berka by Lutheran Pastor Heubel. The interior of the sanctuary looking from the altar toward the organ is pictured on the certificate.

Visitors were drawn to Bad Berka's renowned health spa, which was owned by my stepfather's family. The facility, which was considered luxurious for its time, catered to those with rheumatism and digestive problems. In the complex were eight double guest rooms and four single guest rooms, as well as a mud bath. On staff were two female and two male masseurs. Two different flavors of bottled water were produced at an on-site plant for sale at retail locations.

138

(Above) I couldn't wait for the Ilm River to freeze every winter so my friends and I could go ice skating on it. Our house is visible in the distance beyond the bridge. (Below) I'm pictured with Mutti and Onkel Hans in our yard where my father had planted more than a dozen different varieties of gooseberry bushes.

I had a wonderful time with my new friends at the girls' school in Weimar. We were given lessons on how to cook and bake, but I always found someone else to do my work. I didn't go to those lessons and I never learned the skills that were taught. It was like a game to me. I don't know why the teachers excused me, but they did.

The new dress that I wore to my confirmation (left) served me well when I attended the girls' school in Weimar. Can you pick me out among the students in the top photo?

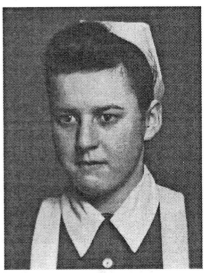

(Top left) Gerhard, a young man I met while working on a German farm, wanted to marry me after the war ended. I laughed off his proposal and felt terribly guilty a short while later when I received an engraved card from his parents announcing his death during the fighting.

(Top right) By the time I became a student nurse in 1944, the hospital was so busy we rarely had time for regular periods of sleep. Gerda, my childhood friend who was also a student nurse, and I took turns sneaking away to nap in out-of-the-way bathtubs.

(Left) After Germany declared war on England, Onkel Hans was assigned a government desk job, but as the ranks of soldiers on the front lines thinned in 1944, he was called up.

(Left) Although Oma Schmidt lived in a house built around 1770 that was attached to the barn, she kept them both very clean and we thought nothing of the arrangement.

When she was a little girl, I could entice my cousin, Inge, (left) who lived with Oma Schmidt, (right) to join me in mischief such as sneaking a midnight snack of cake. This same Oma was so fearless that she picked grass on the hillsides for her rabbits while American fighter planes flew over her head.

CERTIFICATE

INFANTRY · REPLACEMENT
TRAINING · CENTER
FORT McCLELLAN · ALA·

his Certificate
is awarded to···
PVT. HARVEY W. MEINERS
38678923

this 28th day of OCTOBER 19 44 by
the Commanding General of the
· Infantry · Replacement · Training ·
Center · · · · in recognition of his
having successfully completed the
United States Army Basic Training
Cycle.

H. Patrick H. Marvis
Company Commander

*While I was growing up in Bad
Berka, a boy named Harvey Meiners
was growing up in a German family
on a farm near Nechanitz, Texas.
When he received his confirmation
certificate, he had his picture taken
with his maternal grandparents,
(top) Willie and Lina Schellberg
and his paternal grandmother, Sofie
Meiners, about 1933. After Harvey
was called up to serve his country, he
received training in Fort McClellan,
Ala. (above). After graduating from
the infantry program on the 28th of
October 1944, he was first deployed to
Britain and later to Germany (left).*

We heard much propaganda about what would happen to German civilians once the Americans took over our region, but the stories proved to be false. Even though my mother's house was occupied twice by the American army, the soldiers didn't harm us. However, we tried very hard to follow their rules. My friend, Helga, (left) stayed with Mutti and me after the war ended. That's Helga and me in the photo above.

I met Harvey the day
he arrived in Eschwege,
the city where I was
babysitting for Frau Benz.
Thomas Benz, (top left)
whom I looked after, was
a dear child. I am pictured
with Harvey and Frau
Benz at right.

After I got to know Harvey, I looked forward to spending time with him and my upstairs neighbor, Marga, and her GI boyfriend, George (above). George later convinced me that Harvey sincerely cared about me and didn't consider our relationship another fleeting wartime romance. Although they wanted me to come and live with them to help to entertain American officers, Herr and Frau Benz (pictured below) later became friends with Harvey.

Frau Benz thought I should find a more generous boyfriend, an American soldier who could bring us lots of gifts, but I liked Harvey (right). He was a little shy, not so sure of himself like most of the other American soldiers who were part of the U.S. Army of Occupation.

Harvey arranged a place for me to live and found me a job in Fuerstenfeldbruck. For Christmas in 1945, he bought me the best Christmas present I have ever received – a new pair of boots (left). They replaced the ones I had received for my 12th birthday seven years before.

Finally, the papers were all in order and I was officially deNazified. I still find it hard to comprehend that by joining the Jungmaedel as a young girl, I had set in motion the classification that caused us so much heartache. This is our wedding portrait.

Born in Kulmbach, Germany, our darling daughter, Evelyn, was truly a gift from God. (Below at left) My half-sister, Peppi, was saying goodbye to her and Frau Benz is holding Evelyn (below at right).

Onkel Hans and Mutti drove to Nurnberg in their new car to visit us. Evelyn looked so cute in her little hat. How they worshiped that child!

Onkel Hans is pictured above in the yard of my great-grandmother's home in the village of Schoppendorf.

My half-sister, Peppi, and her daughter, Kristel, (left) were sorry to see us go. We thought that perhaps Harvey would decide to stay in Germany, but his mother kept writing asking him when he would return to Texas.

Before we left Germany for America, Evelyn and I crossed the border into the Russian Zone to visit Mutti and Oma Schmidt in Bad Berka. It was the last time I would ever see Oma. Although she never met Harvey, she said if he was good to me and I loved him, I should go back to the U.S. with him.

At 18 months of age, Evelyn attempted to dress herself for the first time (right). She was so happy!

Shortly after Evelyn's birth, Harvey registered our daughter with the American Embassy. On board the freighter to the U.S., Evelyn charmed the crew and other passengers. She had no fear of the water, nor did she suffer from seasickness.

152

When we stepped off the train in Houston, Harvey's sister, Vadie, and her husband, Archie, along with their son, Gary Dean, were there to meet us. A Houston newspaper photographer took our picture and a reporter wrote an article entitled, "Harvey Didn't Waste Time Catching Himself a Girl," which made us all laugh (right).

I was proud to earn my United States citizenship on the 3rd August 1951 (below).

Harvey's family was thrilled when he brought Evelyn and me home to Texas for good. When Evelyn got out of the truck on her first visit to Fayette County, she was so busy chasing the chickens that she hardly had time to meet her grandparents and great-grandparents. In the very first photo we had taken together, at left, she played with Spot, the dog, as Harvey's parents, grandparents and I looked on. It was hard to see my little girl playing in the dirt that afternoon. I was a very particular mother who had a lot to learn about the customs of rural Texas.

Although Fayette County was very different from my home in Germany, I was warmly welcomed by neighbors such as the Matejowsky family, who ran the Nechanitz Store (above). Every month for several years, Charlie Matejowsky helped me package coffee and cigarettes to send Mutti because life was difficult for Germans living in the Russian Zone.

When I went to La Grange, I was prepared to practice my English, but everyone seemed to speak German even at the Fayette County Courthouse (below). Photo courtesy of the Fayette Library and Archives.

Despite feeling terribly homesick, I started the process to help Mutti and Onkel Hans emigrate. Mutti came to the United States first. Later, we were able to bring Onkel Hans. He is pictured (at left) with Evelyn and Harvey at Monument Hill State Park in La Grange and (at left below) with his new car.

Onkel Max, my mother's brother, (below) came to visit us twice on a work visa, but was unable to remain in the U.S., much to his regret and ours.

156

Our daughter, Evelyn, was a beautiful bride when she walked down the aisle with her father (top left). She married the love of her life, John Eldridge Glade, on August 17, 1968, at St. John's Lutheran Church in Houston (top right).

Harvey and I made our first trip back to Germany together in 1971. My family accepted him as if he were one of their own. I liked to tease him that he was more German than I was!

Evelyn wore a traditional Bavarian dirndl costume for her high school German club activities.

When I was confirmed in 1941, I never dreamed that I would emigrate to the U.S. and become an American citizen. Despite living half a world away, I returned to Bad Berka to celebrate the 50th anniversary of my confirmation with other members of my class in 1991 (above). I am standing behind the lady holding the walking cane.

From the day I set foot in Texas, Harvey's family accepted me and treated me with love and respect. Pictured below (left to right) are Harvey's brother, Delvin, and sister, Vadie, along with Harvey and me in 2003. We were celebrating Harvey's 80th birthday.

(Above) It was an honor to be among the six women recognized for their volunteer efforts by the Fayette County Republican Women in July 2013. (At left) Fayette County Republican Women vice president Linda Stall and (center) president Deborah Frank present me with a plaque and roses.

(Below) I was surrounded by my friends (left to right) Christine Wood, Elaine Thomas and Liz Rowden at the pleasant event.

Acknowledgments

Renate is truly an inspiration.

An eyewitness to a fascinating period in world history, she courageously faced the challenges she has encountered in her long life. Renate is a strong and spirited woman of deep faith - traits that became evident to me as she put her past into words and perspective.

Renate's life has been an intriguing and challenging story to tell. During the hundreds of hours I have spent on *Same Moon, Same Stars*, I received valuable input from Christine Wood, Liz Rowden, John Wied, Christa Howells, Darlene Bramblett, Franklin Guettermann, Judy Matejowsky, Shirley Goerlitz, Beth Stier, Carolyn Neely and Aileen Loehr. My husband, Emil, adeptly scanned the majority of the photos that appear in the book. Fred King created a wonderful cover and excellent book design and Irene Prihoda carefully indexed it. I sincerely thank each of you for your insight and enthusiasm for the project.

Working with Renate has been a great privilege. I hope you have learned as much from her life story as she has taught me.

Renate Meiners died Nov. 29, 2014, and is buried in the Waldeck Cemetery in Fayette County, Texas, next to her beloved husband, Harvey.

Elaine Thomas
La Grange, Texas
October 1, 2013

Bibliography

Fugitives of the Forest by Allan Levine, Stoddart Publishing Company, Toronto, Canada, 1998

Gated Grief by Leila Levinson, Cable Publishing, Brule, WI, 2011

World War II Memories by Florence Hertel Farek, Schulenburg Printing, Schulenburg, Texas 1998

Unbelievable Adventures of a WWII German War Bride by Ingeborg M. Johnston, 2010

The Ellen Knauff Story by Ellen Raphael Knauff, W. W. Norton & Company Inc., New York, 1952

War Brides of World War II by Elfrieda Berthiaume Shukert and Barbara Smith Scibetta, Presidio Press, Novato, CA, 1988

Feisty Lydia – Memoirs of a German War Bride (Lydia Ross) by Edna Thayer, Minnesota Heritage Publishing, 2009

Christine, A Novel by Johanna Willner, Authorhouse, 2011

Index